At the Cottage

At the Cottage

*A Fearless Look
at Canada's Summer Obsession*

Charles Gordon

*With Illustrations by
Graham Pilsworth*

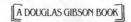
A DOUGLAS GIBSON BOOK

M&S

First published in hardcover 1989
Trade paperback edition 1992

Library and Archives Canada Cataloguing in Publication

Gordon, Charles, 1940–
    At the cottage

ISBN 0-7710-3394-X

1. Vacation homes – Humour. I. Title.

PS8563.0632A95 1989   C813'.54   C89-093473-8
PR9199.3.G662A95 1989

Parts of the following chapters have appeared, in different form, in *The Ottawa Citizen*: "Sort of the 24th of May", and in *Maclean's*: "Good Riddance and When Can We Go Back?", "The Landscape Is Strong", "Still Not the City", and "Great Thoughts With Sunglasses On".

We acknowledge the financial support of the Government of Canada through the Book Publishing Industry Development Program and that of the Government of Ontario through the Ontario Media Development Corporation's Ontario Book Initiative. We further acknowledge the support of the Canada Council for the Arts and the Ontario Arts Council for our publishing program.

Designed by K.T. Njo

Typeset in Janson by M&S, Toronto
Printed and bound in Canada

A Douglas Gibson Book

McClelland & Stewart Ltd.
The Canadian Publishers
481 University Avenue
Toronto, Ontario
M5G 2E9
www.mcclelland.com

4 5 6 7   09 08 07 06 05

Contents

For King and Ruth Gordon,
and for the people at The Lake

Opening

Sort of the 24th of May

Opening

Sort of the 24th of May

Every year, it is the same routine. Load up the car, leaving almost enough room for all the children in the family. And the dog. Drive. Listen to children and dog complaining about over-crowded conditions in the back seat. Drive. Argue about the non-essential stuff that is causing the overcrowded conditions in the back seat and should have been left at home – such as five teddy bears and three bottles of hair conditioner. Drive. Listen to complaints from back seat about absence of sixth teddy bear, which has been left at home.

Drive. Curse the city traffic. Drive some more. Finally reach the country. Curse the country traffic. Drive. Traffic finally gets moving at a reasonable rate. Stop, because somebody is very thirsty, or somebody has to use the bathroom. Or the dog looks like he is about to be sick. Undertake complete unpacking of car, in order to reach dog's leash. Reload car. Resume argument about hair conditioner and excessive number of teddy bears. Drive. Traffic once again at a crawl. Admire scenery, through the rain. Tell children to put down *Archie* comics and admire scenery, if they know what's good for them. Dog gets sick.

✳ ✳ ✳

The road is to the cottage and the day is the 24th of May. Well, not *exactly* the 24th of May, as such. The *weekend* is the 24th of May. And even when it is not, precisely, the 24th of May weekend, it is still called the 24th of May weekend.

It is a long weekend. The actual day of the horrendous drive could be the 21st or 22nd. All that matters is that the Monday of the long weekend be the one preceding the 25th of May. This is the law, has been since 1952. Before that, May 24 was always a holiday no matter what day it was on. Life was simpler in those days, but weekends were shorter.

May 24 was, back in 1819, the day Queen Victoria was born. Early Canadians, for reasons of their own, perhaps because they were Victorians, decided that the day should be a holiday. Later Canadians, noting the invention of the long weekend, decided that something around May 24 would be nice. Parliament, trying to help, decided that May 24 could just as easily be celebrated on the nearest Monday before May 25 and that not only would Queen Victoria's birthday be celebrated but also the birthday of whichever king or queen happened to be reigning at the time – all of which is lost on people in an over-loaded car full of children and hair conditioner and a dog who might be sick again at any moment.

By the end of the 1980s, there were more than half a million vacation homes in Canada. Six per cent of families had one. Using a magical coefficient of 3.2 invented by Statistics Canada, it is possible to estimate that 1,763,200 people are on the highways on this Friday evening. That does not count friends, grandparents, uncles, aunts, dogs, or police officers. It also does not count people who drive trailers, which do not count as vacation homes but count as trailers.

On this weekend that is called the 24th of May weekend even when it isn't, the cars pulling trailers slow down the cars pulling boats, which slow down the cars carrying windsurfers on the roof. Children refuse to enjoy the sight of the rainy countryside and begin arguing over possession of comic books. Dog whimpers. Children, ordered to stop arguing, demand that car stop at roadside stand to buy blueberries. Told that blueberry stands do not open for months, children say: "But they were open *last* year."

The four-lane road becomes a two-lane road, which becomes a dirt road, unimproved since last summer. Worse than last summer. The car, smelling of sick dog, bumps and slides along the washboard. Driver, with no traffic to curse, curses the road. Children, sensing an end to the long ordeal, begin to fight. Dog, sensing an end to the long ordeal, tries to climb out the window, on the driver's side.

Car stops at marina where boat has been stored and serviced to be ready for summer season. Children leap out and continue fighting. Dog finds another dog and sniffs. Groceries, teddy bears, children's ghetto blaster, and a supply of hair conditioner are unloaded, ready for transfer to boat, which is not waiting at dockside. Marina personnel cannot, at first glance, locate boat, but say it must be here somewhere. Two dogs discover they are both male and begin fighting. Children stop fighting and begin crying. Driver yells at everybody to remain calm. Marina informs driver that boat has been found and will be ready in two hours. Driver yells at marina.

✳　　✳　　✳

Following a two-hour picnic in the parking lot of the marina, a picnic punctuated by remarks concerning how cold it is for this time of year, the boat is ready. After an uneventful voyage, the boat, still leaking and still conking out at slow speeds, still doing all the other things it did last year that were supposed to be repaired, arrives at its destination and crashes into the dock. In the semi-darkness, a child slips on the same loose board as last year and scrapes his knee. A parent promises a Band-Aid, once they are inside.

The shutter covering the front door hangs at a funny angle. The door itself is covered with scratches and opens too easily. In the kitchen, unidentifiable bits of something – food perhaps

– cover the floor. Small animal droppings – that is, droppings from a small animal, but droppings nonetheless – are on the floor in the living room, along with the contents of what were once seat cushions.

No Band-Aids are in the medicine cabinet. The child's scraped knee bleeds on the chair that was the subject of last year's argument about whether or not it was a bit too fancy for the cottage. The dog whimpers and hides under the couch. A member of a hardy breed of spring fly buzzes in through gaping holes in a screen.

Half a tree is on the roof. The other half looks like it might soon be. The same selection of canned goods that has been lugged up from the city is found already in the cupboard. By now the lugger's back is sore, as sore as it was at the end of the previous summer. The first baking of the year, carefully covered in waxed paper and put carefully in a box and placed carefully on top of all the other stuff, so as not to get crushed, is crushed.

The cottage, carefully cleaned and swept in September, has to be cleaned and swept again. The pump refuses to fit together, the toilet is making that funny sound again, and the children are refusing to go outside because they saw something large in the woods. Tomorrow the parents will find messes that cannot remotely be identified, but smell bad and have to be cleaned up anyway. The parents will get grease all over themselves trying to fix the pump. They will have to carry the heavy shutters and put them under the house, bumping their heads on things. They will get angry at each other. They know this.

Their backs will get sorer and they will have to jump into water that is colder than it has ever been in the history of the entire lake, partly to get clean, because the pump doesn't work, and partly because the children say it is a "tradition," and if they don't do it they are old. The Stanley Cup finals are on television and there is no television. There is radio. Experience tells them that the game is on the radio, but only in French, and indistinctly at that.

The parents look at each other. "It sure is nice to be here," one says, and means it. The other, to his surprise, agrees.

✳   ✳   ✳

And why? Because it's The Cottage. Or it might be The Cabin, The Shack, The Lake, or The Beach. There are regional variations. In Northern Ontario, around Thunder Bay, people don't go to The Cottage. Cottages are effete eastern creations, for sissies who eat quiche on screened verandas and sip white wine before retiring indoors to watch something on the VCR. Around the head of Lake Superior, people go to Camp.

Albertans near the Rockies go to The Cabin. In Saskatchewan, people go to The Lake. Some Saskatchewan lakes, like Manitoba lakes, are so shallow a swimmer can walk for 100 yards and still be able to touch bottom. Other lakes, farther north, are rocky and deep, though they are still The Lake. In Manitoba, those who do not go to The Lake go to The Beach. In Newfoundland, where there is a sea but hardly a beach, many people go to The Shack – those who are not fortunate enough to go to a Summer Home. British Columbians, who have beaches, and sea, and lakes, go to The Cabin. Many Torontonians go North; Ottawans go to The Gatineau. And everyone goes, at some point, to something called "Our Summer Place."

Whatever it is called, wherever it is, it is probably a cottage, at least in the dictionary sense:

"1. A small house, usually of only one storey; 2. a small, modest house at a lake, mountain resort, etc., owned or rented as a vacation home . . . – Syn. 1, 2. COTTAGE, CABIN, LODGE, SHACK, HUT, SHANTY. Formerly meant small, simple, often crude dwellings. During recent years, the first four words have gained great currency as terms for the often elaborate structures maintained by the well-to-do for recreational purposes. HUT and SHANTY still have the former meaning as their most frequent one."

Whether it is a cottage, cabin, shack, or lodge, or whether it is camp, it is probably near a body of water, usually a lake. It has fewer creature comforts than its urban, suburban, or even rural counterpart. It has more bugs, less lawn, at least one boat, at least one mouse, a smaller kitchen, a larger birdhouse. Neighbours are farther away. So are stores. There may be a road to it; it may be accessible only by water. Either way, it is harder to get to than the place people live in the rest of the year.

That may be its charm. It is hard to get to. It is hard for *other people* to get to. The telephone doesn't ring, either because there isn't one, or because hardly anyone knows the number. Carpet cleaning companies and chimney sweeping establishments don't, anyway. Nor do magazine subscription departments, political parties, friends of teen-agers.

Cars don't go by. Boats do, but not as frequently as cars would if the lake were a road. Trucks never go by. Large airplanes fly overhead, but at considerable altitude. The Cottage is not on the glide path. The only planes in the vicinity are small ones that sound the way planes should.

Once, the Cottage was wilderness. Once it was solitude. Now it is neither. But it is still closer to wilderness, closer to solitude than the city is. There may be fewer fish, fewer hawks and fewer foxes than there used to be, but there are still more than there are in the city. For all the headaches and expense, for all the machines that don't work and animals that tear holes in the screen, the cottage is still . . . well, different.

There is variety in the cottages and their settings. There are deep mountain lakes, rocky Ontario lakes, and shallow prairie lakes. The old wooden cottage on Georgian Bay that's been in the family for three generations is different from the three-generation place beside a lake in the Eastern Townships; the main house at Port Joli in southern Nova Scotia is not the same as the main house at Clear Lake in western Manitoba. The cottage in Muskoka is different from the one at Greenwater Lake in Saskatchewan. That one is different from the one in the Lake of the Woods, and that one is different from the one on the Gatineau River in Quebec. The shack in Newfoundland is different from the cabin in British Columbia. There are sweeping structures of cedar and glass and humble loggers' cabins with old rags stuffed into the cracks. But the cottage mentality lives in each; elements of the cottage experience stretch from coast to coast. What each structure and each setting offers is another way of living.

The other way of living has its own sounds and smells. That's why people are back again this year, despite having to carry water up from the lake when the pump doesn't work, despite having to sweep up miscellaneous animal leavings, despite having to take the shutters off and risk further injury to backs. The cottage is different.

Part 1

Things You Should Know About

Supplies
There Is No Escaping the Law of Flashlights
Decor
The National Fabric Is Torn, But the Hell with It
Weather
Sooner or Later You Have to Go Outside
Pain
Is Putting Your Back Out Worse than a Hornet?
Power
Remembering the Days Before Garlic Was Electric
Water
That Rock Wasn't There Last Year
Wilderness
It's a Jungle in There

Supplies

There Is No Escaping the Law of Flashlights

One important thing to remember when preparing for the cottage is not to take too much. Another important thing to remember is not to take too little.

The quantity of supplies people bring with them indicates one of two main views of cottage life: either they are completely leaving civilization for a few weeks, or they are just shifting to another part of it. You can tell someone who holds the first view as soon as they ask certain tell-tale questions, such as: "Do they have Kleenex up there?"

Boxes of Kleenex tumble from the dozens of grocery bags carried by such a person. Their grocery bags also contain:

24 bars of soap
30 tubes of toothpaste
9 bottles of shampoo
37 packages of dried soup
2 cases of canned vegetables
15 cans of coffee
winter boots
15 boxes of tea
some mosquito netting.

The advantages of this approach to supplying the cottage should not be underestimated:

1. There is no need to buy Kleenex for five years.
2. There is no need to buy dried soup for ten years.
3. Toothpaste lasts indefinitely.
4. You never know when you might need mosquito netting.

The disadvantages are slightly more numerous:

1. The stuff has to be unloaded from the car.
2. It has to be carried up the hill.
3. It has to be unloaded at the cottage.
4. No one knows where to put 30 tubes of toothpaste.
5. At midsummer, 25 tubes of toothpaste are open at the same time.

There are other problems. The entire procedure has to be repeated in reverse at summer's end, and it is now uphill to the car, for some reason. (Those who cannot go directly from car to cottage have even more work ahead of them, adding the cottage-to-boat and boat-to-car stages, each of them mysteriously uphill.) And by a puzzling physical process, canned vegetables are heavier at summer's end than at summer's beginning.

Overloading with canned vegetables also leads to difficult arguments that increase the weight of the supplies that have to be carried back to the car. In most cases, the person responsible for the carrying and loading of the surplus canned vegetables argues that they can be left in the pantry over the winter, safe from spoilage, safe from the prying claws of the various beasts that enjoy vegetables in the off-season. Sometimes the person responsible for the loading of the canned vegetables even argues that beasts do not like vegetables at all in the winter months, preferring bark and dead mice.

The person responsible for the purchase of the canned vegetables argues that they will explode if left over the winter, the explosion being caused by contractions and expansions in response to freezing and thawing and whatnot. If allowed to happen, this explosion will cause bits of peas and corn to be flung all over the inside of the cottage, breaking windows and attracting animals from miles around who will, in combination with the rotting vegetables themselves, create a horrible smell.

Excesses in the fruit, vegetable, and household supplies are not the only examples of overpacking. Many is the rookie would-be carpenter and outdoorsman who arrives carrying bricks, boards, and flat rocks. And if you look into his suitcase, you will find seven sweaters, five bathing suits, all his shirts, five ties, a dinner jacket (just in case), and six pairs of shoes.

It is natural that first-time cottage people think of themselves as travelling to a place where the nearest store is twenty-five miles away and sells only rope. It is only natural also that others arrive with nothing but suntan lotion and dinner for tonight, it being their thought that they will just nip over to the store for whatever else they might need. In such cases, the store is always ten miles away, through the rain and heavy wind, in a boat driven by someone who grits her teeth and says she doesn't mind at all.

This is especially bad if the commodity being sought is cigarettes. Invariably, the driver of the boat through the rain and over – and under – the high waves is a person who smiles and says he understands: he used to smoke himself.

※　　※　　※

So what *do* you need? A good way of deciding is to remember what you will and won't find at the Cottage. You will find bugs. You won't find heat. You may not find light, and even if there is light, it may go out in a thunderstorm.

You may not find television, or a radio station that can bring in the ball game. Other things you must be prepared not to find include newspapers, a freezer, a dishwasher, a washing machine, a microwave oven, and a neighbour with lots of tools.

So here are some things you will need. In selecting supplies, remember that certain staples that are never consumed in the city become necessities at the cottage. One is Kool-Aid. The other one is cookies. Store-bought ones will do in a pinch. The rest of the list:

Food, of course.
Flashlight batteries.
Candles.
At least two decks of cards, with the jokers.
Extra screening.
A hammer, some screwdrivers, some screws and nails.
Mystery books.
A crowbar.
A shirt you can get paint on.
A saw.
A dog, if you can find one that doesn't bark.
Children and other relatives, up to a point.
Things that stop itching.
Your second-best running shoes.
Sunglasses.
Extra sunglasses.
A hat you can get paint on.
Some jeans with pockets.
All the socks and underwear you own.
Knitting.
A jigsaw puzzle.

Although flashlight batteries are on the list, flashlights are not. Unless you are opening a cottage for the first time, the flashlights are supposed to be there. The fact that they are not does not change that fact. It is a difficult problem to solve because the Law of Flashlights states that the number of flashlights varies in inverse proportion to the availability of batteries. The recommendation that you bring batteries guarantees that there will be no flashlights there. On the other hand, a recommendation that you bring flashlights almost certainly means that something will happen to the batteries.

It is too bad this always happens, because flashlights are

handy to have for getting around outside in the dark and are great fun for kids to play with under the covers when they are supposed to be asleep and you are looking for a flashlight.

Stamps and stationery are regarded by many as essential items. This is because you have the time at the cottage to write all the letters you wanted to write over the winter. Without stamps and stationery you will never get those letters written. However, the time you have to write all the letters you wanted to write over the winter is also the time you have to read all the books you wanted to read over the winter. Plus, there are the demands of children, relatives, and the dog that doesn't bark, as well as the necessity of taking a little nap every now and then. But think how bad you'd feel if you were suddenly struck with the urge to write a letter and didn't have anything to write it on.

The letter could be serious. You might be writing to invite a guest up for the weekend and asking the guest to bring more flashlight batteries.

Decor

The National Fabric Is Torn
But the Hell with It

New owners inevitably try to do too much. They see what a wreck the place is. They see beyond the wreck and see their dream cottage. That is their first mistake. A cottage should not look like a dream cottage. A cottage is going to have wet towels, an opened package of Oreo cookies, and some *Archie* comics lying on the floor. Dream cottages never look like that.

Dream cottages come from magazines. They have decks, and people sit on them wearing outfits and sipping things out of frosted glasses. There are raw vegetables at the dream cottage. There is a dip. There are places to put wet towels so that no one can see them. All the furniture has bright yellow fabric covering it. There are no heads of animals mounted on the wall, only a barometer that works and a nice antique drawing of a three-masted schooner.

A first-time cottage owner leafing through such a magazine could be misled, particularly by the picture spreads showing how to convert that tacky old wreck into a tasteful masterpiece. The most important thing to remember about such a conversion is that it would be a grave mistake. Cottages are not meant to be trendy. Their purpose is to keep out, for the most part, the rain and the mosquitoes, and to enshrine the household flotsam and jetsam of preceding generations.

The well-meaning new cottage owner will, after reading the magazines, paint the walls a bright colour, thus violating one of the primary rules of cottage design: The inside of a cottage is supposed to be dark. This is partly so that it will be cool on hot days. But there is also a more important reason. If the inside of the cottage is dark, then it will be really dark on rainy days, allowing you no choice but to play Monopoly, using mismatched dice and acorns for hotels.

A second point to remember about redecorating cottages is that cottages are not like city apartments. In city apartments, it is customary to hang plants from the ceiling. People do this because there are no other plants around. In summer cottages, there are other plants around, namely trees and poison ivy. Therefore it is redundant – possibly even dangerous – to hang plants inside. There are lots of other plants outside that were there before the hanging plants arrived. What will they think?

A cottage will collect junk. It is a natural quality of cottages that they do so. Junk looks terrible in a tastefully decorated cottage. It looks out of place. A cottage should never make junk look out of place. Junk, like trophies, must be displayed.

Many new cottage owners do not know it, but there *will* be trophies. Every lake within easy reach of a large city has an association whose main purpose is to award trophies on long weekends. The trophies are for finishing fourth, for showing up, for not drowning, for not tipping over, for only tipping over once, for being the oldest, for showing up two years in a row, and for not getting trophies for anything else. Such trophies can add up over the course of a summer, particularly if there are several children. They must be kept. Children do not throw away trophies easily, and adults, who still think of trophies in terms of finishing *first* and therefore regard them with a certain amount of awe, won't throw them away either.

There have to be shelves to put the trophies on, shelves separate and distinct from the shelves holding the previous owner's trophies, which cannot be thrown out because they are part of the heritage of the cottage. Devoting shelves to trophies inevitably means that shelves cannot be devoted to plants. Moving plants onto kitchen shelves can be only a short-term solution. In the kitchen, the plants will displace the collection of exotic spices that will never be used for cottage cooking but look nice. Eventually, however, even those shelves will be needed for trophies.

The shortage of shelf space raises the question of what should be done with the junk the previous owner left around. The answer is that it is the new owner's duty to keep it. It is part of the cottage owner's code: to keep it, and to keep it where it was.

This has to do with the national fabric, which no new cottage owner would want to rend in any way. A lot of cottage stuff is inextricably interwoven into the national fabric. Some of it is not, but it is difficult to tell which cottage junk falls into the inextricably interwoven category and which is only junk. The safe thing to do is to keep it all. In these unstable, perhaps even parlous, times, it is essential to the nation's future that there be a degree of continuity in the way the nation looks. In the summertime, the nation always puts out teacups celebrating a not very recent royal visit. It scatters ashtrays commemorating Expo '67 and a visit to Dayton, Ohio. It has a 45-rpm phonograph record by Frankie Laine, even though there was never a phonograph in the cottage. It hangs torn posters celebrating the joys of Weimar Republic Germany, peaceful Northern Ireland, and a petrified forest somebody visited once in a state beginning with the letter *I*.

The nation sits on wicker armchairs that list to starboard. It reclines on chesterfields too lumpy for the city. It lies back on couches that swing back and forth on squeaking chains.

Cottage Nation reads magazines whose covers proclaim the unwavering love of Eddie and Debbie. It saves, for future reference, the June 11, 1984, edition of *Time* magazine, whose cover proclaims "Why Pain Hurts," plus "El Salvador gets a new president" and "Mondale, Hart and Jackson struggle through the final round."

At the cottage, the nation proudly displays a yard or two of Reader's Digest Condensed Books and, on the floor beside the once-floral patterned sofa, a pre–Travis McGee work by John D. MacDonald, with page 52 missing, sacrificed for some now unremembered cause.

In covering all this over with teak and shag carpet, the new cottage owners are messing with powerful forces they don't understand.

Weather

Sooner or Later You Have to Go Outside

You may not be exactly roughing it out there, but you are closer to nature than you were on the twelfth storey of a downtown high-rise, or in the fifth identical house to the left on a suburban street named after a flowering shrub.

When you are closer to nature the weather matters, all of a sudden. Sure, you're not a pioneer. You're not laying trap lines and chasing down rabbits for food. You can go inside when you want to and turn up the heat, if you have heat to turn up. If you don't have heat to turn up, you can put another log on the fire. But the weather is out there, and sooner or later you are going to have to go out in it.

In the city, the weather is something you have to sit through before the sports comes on. If it rains, you get a couple of drops on you on the way to the car or the bus. If it rains, your golf game has to be put back a day, the children have to be reminded to put their jackets on, and the grass doesn't have to be cut. If it doesn't rain, the garden won't grow. But the garden is mostly for recreation anyway, and if it happens to be intended to grow vegetables and the weather prevents the garden from doing so, well, vegetables can always be bought at the supermarket.

Summer storms rarely amount to much in the city, and if

a big one hits the main concern is whether it affected the cable television reception or caused the computer at the bank to go down. Other weather-associated phenomena have even less impact. There are rumoured to be sunsets in some cities, but they are usually well hidden behind apartment buildings.

At the cottage, the weather is everything. It affects the work that can be done. It determines what the children will do. It influences the fishing and all aspects of recreational life. It is the first topic of conversation. And it lives on in history. The year 1988, when people look back on it, will not be known as the year of *Glasnost* or the year Gretzky was traded to Los Angeles, but as the year the summer was so hot.

If it is hot, you spend a lot of time on the dock working on your tan. If it is too hot, the fishing is no good. If it rains, the danger of forest fires diminishes, the berries grow, and the bears are likely to stay away from the garbage. Also, if it rains, the July woodsmen are going to be grumpy because they don't get to take their chain saws outside, the kids are going to be playing cards in the living room, yelling and causing the seven of spades to be missing from the deck when you try to play cribbage with it later on.

If there is a thunderstorm, a tree might be struck and fall over, causing either damage to the roof or a year's supply of firewood, or both. If there is a high wind, all the towels are going to blow away, everything has to be moved off the veranda, and the boat trip for groceries is going to be risky. The old-timers – that is to say, those thirty-five or older – will trot out their tales of sailboats that were struck by lightning, inboards that were swamped by high waves, and outboards that were never seen again. Various local superstitions will come into play, such as the one about milk going sour when there is lightning within a seven-mile radius.

Everything depends on the weather. People who don't care about the Expos, the political situation, or even the survival of the planet as we know it today turn on their transistor radios every day at dawn to find out if it will be nice or not. People who can't be bothered to read the newspapers because they think news should not be allowed to take place during July and August sneak a glance at the weather page and attempt to make sense of it. (They can only make an attempt, because the place they happen to be is never included in the forecasts, forcing them to examine the forecast for the nearest area and guess which way the weather will travel when it is through with being the weather in the area referred to in the newspaper.)

For thoughtful people, of whom there are a few on the lake every year, closeness to the weather has a soothing effect. The stock market may be up, the government's standing in the polls may be down, hemlines may be lower and French wine prices higher – but none of it matters as much as whether the sun comes out and the rain stops. And no person, not even a government, can make that happen. This is a humbling thought, and more people should have it.

Because everything depends on the weather, there are several things the novice cottager should understand about it. The first is how to read those newspaper forecasts.

"MUSKOKA-HALIBURTON (or BANFF–LAKE LOUISE)," the forecast says. "Today will bring clouds and some sunshine with a shower or thundershower. Highs 19–21. Tonight will be cool; it may shower early, then some cloudiness will occur. Lows 10–12. Tomorrow will bring intervals of clouds and sunshine, but it should remain dry. Highs 20–22. Sunday will bring more damp weather."

The forecast is accompanied by three mysterious illustrations, which appear to show, respectively, the sun peeping out from behind the moon, raindrops falling from the sun and lightning bolts shooting up from clouds. The drawings have a contemporary look to them and have probably been done by a computer.

But this is not your main difficulty in seeking to make sense of the forecast. Your main difficulty is that you don't happen to be in Muskoka or Haliburton or anywhere in between that could be classified as Muskoka-Haliburton. You are about a hundred miles away, or more, depending upon whether your main reference point is Muskoka or Haliburton, both of them being pretty large reference points anyway. You are not sure quite where you are except that you're not in TORONTO-HAMILTON, in which case you'd still be on the twelfth floor of an apartment building. So the best thing you can do is read through the part about MUSKOKA-HALIBURTON and figure you'll be getting something like that at some stage, unless it's going the other way.

So none of this is much help. As for highs being 19–21, some people don't care about this. They say all that matters is whether it feels warm or not. Other people call in their children, who are familiar with the metric system and can say whether 19–21 is hot or cold.

And as for tonight being cool, this will affect eating plans – indoors or out – and is important. But it is not cool right now, and the question is how long will it take the coolness in Muskoka-Haliburton to reach here, or whether the evening coolness predicted for Muskoka-Haliburton was really the morning coolness we already had here, so we don't have to worry about it any more. These are important judgement calls, and a mistake, such as scheduling a picnic in the middle of coolness, will be greeted by cries of "Didn't you read the forecast?"

"*Tomorrow will bring intervals of cloud and sunshine, but it should remain dry. Sunday will bring more damp weather.*" This is the part that you really read the forecast for. Most of today is past by the time the paper arrives, but tomorrow is, as they say, another day and an outing is planned. "It says here," you say, looking up from the newspaper, "that tomorrow will bring intervals of cloud and sunshine."

"What's that mean?"

"I think it means it isn't going to rain."

"Is intervals of cloud and sunshine more cloudy than intervals of sunshine and cloud?"

"How the hell should I know?"

"Do you think we should go ahead with the picnic?"

"I don't know. Wait a second. It says Sunday will bring more damp weather. That must mean it's going to be damp Saturday if Sunday is going to bring more."

"But you said it's not going to rain Saturday."

"That's what the paper says. It says 'it should remain dry.' "

"Let's see what it looks like in the morning."

"OK."

❋　❋　❋

There are other things the cottage novice should understand about the weather:

• *The weather at dawn will never be seen again if it is good.* If you awaken at dawn with the sun streaming through the window and a marvellous sunrise breaking over the horizon, you should always get up and enjoy it. If you go back to sleep, in the expectation of a sunny day, you will wake up to clouds, and worse. Cottage scientists, of whom there is no shortage, have labelled this the Dawn Hypothesis.

It is unlikely that your going back to sleep actually *causes* clouds, but no theory should be discounted. If it is cloudy at dawn and you go back to sleep, it will also be cloudy during the day. So you may cause the clouds by going back to sleep. Or you may cause the clouds by waking up at dawn. There are all kinds of theories and who is to know. There is a cottage where lives a beautiful woman who is convinced that the wind always stops when the sun sets. She does not say that the setting sun actually *causes* the wind to diminish. Nor would she go so far as to say that the diminishing wind causes the sun to set. She just points to the correlation between the two, and who is to say that she is wrong?

You can test the Dawn Hypothesis yourself by making sure not to wake up early. Many cottagers have become quite adept at this.

• *The weather is never the same as it was before.* This should be obvious. People never sit around the table and say, "We always have weather like this." They say, "I can't remember when it's been this cloudy (or this cold, or this hot, or this damp, or this humid)." When you think about it, it is extraordinary that there has never been weather like this before, given how few kinds of weather there are and how many years there have been. There are only two basic types of weather, not counting snow, which no one wants to. These are: (1) Raining and (2) Not raining.

These two types can be broken into several sub-types:

1. Cold and raining.
2. Cold and not raining.
3. Hot and not raining.
4. Cold and just stopped raining.
5. Hot and about to rain.
6. Cold and about to rain.
7. Not likely to rain at all, although you never know.

That still leaves only seven different kinds of weather. The odds are these are going to repeat themselves frequently. Yet people claim they never do. "There has never been a summer like this." "I can't remember there ever being a week like this." "There has never been a storm like that." "It's never been this hot." A mathematical phenomenon is at work here, which mathematicians would be well advised to pay attention to, instead of spending all their time trying to make pi come out even.

• *The weather was more like this during the War.* This is a related theory. While no one can remember the weather being exactly like this in the short term, the weather was exactly like this during the War, *only more so.* The older cottagers remember, and who would quarrel with them?

If you think this is hot, they will say, you should have seen it during the War. It was just like this, except it was hotter. People were frying eggs on the dock, it was so hot. Of course, the eggs we had then are not the same as the eggs you have now.

Many of the older cottagers remember the weather during the Great Depression as well. As you can imagine, there was nothing great about it. It was more cloudy than this and months would go by without the rain letting up. Reminded of the drought conditions prevalent in those days, the older cottagers will suggest that it was probably because the cottage got all the rain that there was not enough left for the prairies.

• *The weather becomes tiresome.* It is easy to get tired of the rain. The men begin drinking earlier and earlier in the day. The children's quarrels over the Monopoly game become increasingly physical. The cottage floor becomes covered with muddy footprints and no baking can be done because all the bowls are on the floor catching leaks from the roof. But it is worth remembering that glorious weather becomes boring too.

People are never satisfied. Give them a solid week of high temperatures, sunshine, light winds, low humidity, and warm water and they begin complaining. "I wish we'd get just one rainy day so I could sit inside and read a book," they say. Or they disguise their boredom in loftier motives: "The moss is drying out. It would be nice if it could get a little rain."

After two weeks of sunshine and sun-tanning, people are on edge. Their anxiety over peeling reaches the danger point. They begin seeing clouds on the horizon, which they eagerly point out, only to discover the clouds were just smudges on their sunglasses. The water is too warm, all of a sudden.

"It isn't even refreshing," someone will say.

"I can't sleep in this weather," someone will add.

When the storm breaks, as eventually it must, they will welcome it for a while. Then the first leaks will come through the roof and the first whines will come from the first child.

"I'm bored," the first child will say. "I want to go outside."

"You can't go outside," the first child's mother will say. "It's raining."

"When's it going to stop raining?" the first child will ask.

• *There are weather optimists and weather pessimists.* Watch two people look at the sky. One of them, usually a man, looks up and sees clouds. "I think it's going to be a three-day blow," he says. The other one, often a woman, looks at the same sky.

"There's enough blue there to make a Dutchman's britches," she says.

People read the sky differently and their reading reflects what they want. The man doesn't want to start up the chain saw. He doesn't want to paint the boathouse. He wants rain, so he can sit inside, drink coffee, and sort out the plugs in his tackle box.

The woman wants sun. She wants the children out of the house. She doesn't want muddy footprints in the kitchen and she doesn't want fishing plugs all over the dining room table.

There are, in addition, natural optimists and natural pessimists. The natural pessimist is afraid that things will go wrong. He thinks they will hurt him less if he expects them. There are documented cases of men who have predicted storms *every single day* of their vacation. For such a man, the storm, when it arrives, is vindication. The sunshine, when it unaccountably puts in an appearance, is a pleasant surprise. Pessimism makes a kind of sense. There is little accounting for optimism.

Disagreements about the weather are not unpleasant. In fact, they are necessary. They provide a sure-fire topic of conversation for breakfast, dinner, and supper tables. Without the weather, the table would fall silent, since no one has the faintest idea what's in the newspapers.

Pain

Is Putting Your Back Out Worse than a Hornet?

When you were a kid at the cottage and you hurt something, someone would explain the pain to you, and that's the way you remembered it all through your life, even if it was wrong.

The itchy red mark on your arm was a spider bite. It could have been a mosquito bite, but it felt better for being a spider bite. Spider bites were not available in the city. You thought of how you would tell your friends. The spiders could crawl right inside your sleeping bag and up your leg and bite you.

Cottage bee stings were worse than city ones too, because you never knew where they were coming from. City bee stings came from bees. The bees hung around the flowers doing something and if you bothered them they stung you. Everybody knew that. Whereas cottage bees hid out in dead logs and stumps, or they made nests under the roof of the old icehouse. You had to be careful every minute you were tramping through the bush because at any time, just when you didn't expect it, pow! One of those bees would get you.

And it might be worse than a bee too. It might be a hornet. Hornets were worse than bees. The pain you got from a hornet was at least fifty times worse than a bee. And it was two hundred times worse than you got from a wasp.

After the initial pain and shock had gone away, it was a good idea to establish what it was that had caused it, in order to furnish those important details that make the difference between a good story and a great one. This could take some time, because of regional differences in the identification of the various types of stinging insects. What some people called a yellow jacket – small, yellow; not a bad stinger, but no hornet – other people called a wasp; whereas other people thought a wasp was a slow-moving black thing that could hardly sting at all and mostly hung around in bathrooms in farming areas.

There were ordinary bumblebees, about which there was no argument, and there were hornets. Most people agreed on hornets. They were black and white and they stung like crazy. Your arm, where it got stung, would swell up to twenty times its normal size, and sometimes you'd have to be taken to the hospital to have someone look at it and give you a prescription for a powerful antibiotic.

That's how bad it was with hornets. The other thing about hornets was they travelled in packs. Packs of wild hornets. And if one of them stung you then they'd all sting you. You and all your relatives would have to go racing down the side of a hill where there was no path, screaming and trying to get away from the hornets.

Sometimes you could step on a root, fall and twist your ankle. That could hurt a lot, but there was no pain like a hornet.

The cottage has its own unique brand of pain, pain that cannot be found in the city, pain that lives on in memory, making marks on the calendar. The summer of '59 – that was the year you pulled your shoulder out of its socket waterskiing, wasn't it? Don't be stupid: I didn't pull it out of its socket; I just strained it a little bit. Well, Dad said you pulled it out of its socket and I believed him.

In cottage legend, shoulders are pulled out of sockets, feet swell and life-long trick knees are developed. Back pain, while less picturesque, often occurs several times on the calendar. The summer the new dock was built – '72, remember? – you couldn't help and spent all your time sitting in a chair watching, because you'd hurt your back waterskiing.

While almost all back pain suffered by Cottage Man is the result of his lifting too large a log all by himself to demonstrate how strong he is, there are several types.

1. Real back pain, the result of lifting too large a log to demonstrate how strong you are.

2. Apprehended back pain, existing in the minds of those who tell you not to lift that log because you will hurt your back doing it.

3. Chronic back pain, which the people who have it have always had – at least, they already have it when they arrive at the cottage and, unfortunately, it prevents them from helping out as much as they'd like.

It is difficult to pinpoint when the pain began for chronic back pain sufferers, other than it began some time before their arrival. It is characteristic of those afflicted with this tragic condition that they don't inform their hosts of their chronic back pain before they arrive. This is because they don't want their hosts to go to any extra trouble, in the way of ordering special mattresses and whatnot.

Some chronic back pain sufferers, more daring than others, will attempt to pitch in with the chores. But in doing so, they are always risking the condition known to the layman as "putting my back out." No one knows exactly how it happens, but thousands of people, each summer, suddenly put their backs out. "Oh damn," one will say, straightening up, slowly, from the task, "I've put my back out."

He then goes inside to rest, groaning loudly, and somebody brings him a glass of cold lemonade. The groans create some excitement for the children, who rush to the side of the back sufferer. He is forced to explain to the children that he did not, literally, put his back out – that is, he did not put it out the door, like you would put the cat out or hang a wet towel out. While the work goes on outside, he will further explain to the children that the pain associated with putting your back out is intense, but lying down, or at least sitting still, will help it go away. The children will want to know if the pain is worse than a hornet.

* * *

Waterskiing pain is sudden, frightening, and tied up with the fear of speed, broken limbs, and, for those who ski with their contact lenses out, the unknown. Path-clearing pain is gradual, irritating, an accumulation of little scratches from branches and thorns that grab at your knees. Since you always clear a path on the spur of the moment, you are never wearing long pants when you do it.

Other pain exists mainly in anticipation. City children learn to place their feet apart when they swing an axe into a chopping block. They are told that the axe will go right into their foot if their legs are not spread wide. Even as they grow up, their feet moving a bit closer together and their stances becoming a bit less exaggerated, they can almost feel the axe hitting the foot. Every once in a while, the blade will bounce off a length of wood at a funny angle, or miss the block altogether, and the chopper, who has somehow managed to avoid chopping himself, will feel the pain that he has never really felt.

Another pain that is mostly imaginary is the fish hook embedded in the thumb. Stories are told about people forced to live out their lives with red-and-white Lazy Ikes stuck in their thumb. Their social lives are ruined, apparently, because of this, and the horror of their wedding nights is best left to the imagination. None of the people who tell the stories has actually met one of these unfortunate individuals, but they know someone who knew someone who has. Every time a young fisherman pricks himself with a hook, he shudders and feels a legendary pain.

Bloodsucker pain is legendary as well. Although the bloodsucker is the tiniest and most inoffensive-looking creature, the merest hint of one in the water can send children and grown men leaping to dry ground. The appearance of a leech – a considerably larger and nastier-looking creature, which generations have been told don't suck your blood anyway – can cause mild panic. Yet the actual sucking of blood, when it occurs, is nothing. It's not even as bad as a wasp.

This tiny black thing just sits there, between your toes. Nevertheless, it is cause for alarm. Ancestral stories about blood-suckers are recalled, about people who went for weeks with one of those little devils between their toes; the people who gradually lost colour and were subject to fainting spells. Only at the eleventh hour was a specialist able to find and eradicate the cause. By this time, the bloodsucker was three storeys high and had turned a bright red.

Such stories send the family scurrying for the salt, an ancient remedy. Salt, liberally dumped upon it, will cause the tiny black creature to withdraw its bloodsucking head from the wound, whereupon it can be pulled off and buried in the sand. Failing salt, the lit end of a cigarette will do the job. Lately, with the sudden dearth of cigarette smokers, salt has made a comeback, and not a moment too soon.

What sustains Cottage Man in his pain is the thought that he will be able to tell a good story about it when he is back in the city. In that context, certain types of pain are more useful than others. Pain accompanied by heroism – or at least a certain basic dignity – is the best. Take, as an example, falling down. The pain of falling down is real, but falling down can happen anywhere and is not usually accomplished gracefully, although there is a certain drama to falling halfway through a rotten board on the roof. Similarly, hammer wounds, while real and painful, are low in storytelling value, unless they can be shown to have occurred in noble circumstances, such as in clinging to the edge of a thirty-foot-high cabin roof while unsuccessfully hammering a roofing nail and successfully hammering a thumb.

Cottage pain too often lacks dignity. There is nothing in the slightest bit redeeming about bruising your bottom when you fall against a seat in the outboard after the cord you are pulling to start the motor breaks, sending you lurching towards the bow with a broken cord in your hand. A lack of dignity has also befallen sunburn, that most common of cottage wounds. Since it has been linked by the media to skin cancer and self-indulgence, no one brags about sunburn now, any more than they would brag about noses rubbed sore by excessive Kleenex application during hay fever attacks. As a topic, sunburn does not even deserve to be in the same room as chronic back pain. The backbone is still the backbone of cottage conversation.

Power

Remembering the Days
Before Garlic Was Electric

When the electricity came, everybody was delighted. Everybody but an old grouch or two. But there were always old grouches around. Name anything, name any one thing, and the old grouches would tell you it was better before.

The food was better in the old days. They made better nails then. The old wooden boats were better than these new aluminum jobs. A two-by-four was a two-by-four. Things didn't fall apart in the old days. This new music can't touch the stuff we danced to in the old days. And dancing. You call that dancing that they do now? The lake was better in the old days. It was cleaner and quieter. The water was clearer. The store had things you needed, instead of plastic geegaws for the tourists. The people were friendlier. Even the *trees* were better in the old days.

A person did not have to be old to be an old grouch. A few old grouches were in their teens. Many of them were under forty. Old grouch-hood was less an age than a state of mind. No matter what his or her age, an old grouch would carry on during discussions of things like the coming of electricity. But people were used to it. Old grouches had always carried on, and people could see what the electricity would mean. No more lighting the lamps. No more carrying in wood for the stove.

Hot water. Power tools. Vacuuming instead of sweeping. Maybe even (although no one would say it too loud at first) a dishwasher.

Life would be easier – safer too, because people wouldn't be swinging axes all the time. They'd be spending less time with the chain saw and there wouldn't be the need to have all that kerosene around for the lamps. With electricity, you could have a pump that went on automatically whenever anyone turned on the tap or flushed the toilet.

With electricity you could have toilets!

You would never run out of water. You could throw away the big ugly water tank at the top of the hill. You could throw away the noisy gasoline pump that filled the big ugly water tank at the top of the hill.

Every room could have a little electric heater in it, so that it wouldn't be so cold to get up in the morning. Reading would be easier. People's eyes wouldn't go bad. There could be electric blankets. There could be electric kettles, electric irons – any number of helpful and practical electric things.

When the electricity came, life was very nice for a while. The electric kettle was good and there was even an electric coffee grinder, so the coffee was better than it was before the electricity came. People enjoyed reading more than they used to and the old grouches, who liked to read – particularly newspaper articles about how bad things were today – didn't complain for a while.

Contrary to what the old grouches had been warning, people didn't vegetate. There was still lots of physical work to do, such as dismantling the old pump, taking apart the big tank and getting rid of it, and tearing down the old outhouse. In addition, the new power tools were kept busy making cupboards and brackets to hold some of the new electric appliances.

There were a few extra of those. The thing was, if you kept getting labour-saving devices for Christmas and they weren't much good to you in the city, you might as well make use of them somewhere. In addition to the electric coffee grinder, soon there was the electric can opener, the electric knife sharpener, which wasn't really needed because of the electric carving knife, but anyway it was there–there was no point in leaving it in the city. The frying pan was electric now. And there was something else, another Christmas present, and no one knew exactly what it was, but it was there. Somebody thought it was an electric garlic press. This got one of the old grouches going about the days before garlic was electric.

Until the television set appeared, the old grouches didn't complain too loudly. They just muttered to themselves occasionally. The sound of the vacuum cleaner bothered them and they would talk beneath the whine, recalling the days when the women swept and chatted while they swept and what a pleasant sound it was, particularly if you didn't have to be one of them.

It may have been to counter the noise the old grouches made that the television set was first brought in. But more likely it was a special occasion, a one-shot deal. Somebody remembers it was a royal wedding; somebody else thinks it was the Olympic Games. Whatever it was, the occasion was so special, so non-recurring, that advocates of the television set could say this:

"Look, this doesn't mean we're going to have television in the cottage. It doesn't mean the children will spend all their time watching cartoons. It doesn't mean that game shows are going to be on all afternoon. It doesn't mean we'll have to watch baseball games and wrestling. It's just for this one thing. Then we'll take it back."

That first TV set experience varies among cottage people. One couple remembers dragging a large colour television set, advertised as portable, out of an outboard motor boat, up a large hill and into a house, installing it and adjusting the picture, only to have the power go out on the day Charles married Diana. A woman remembers convincing her husband to spend a golden autumn weekend at the cottage only by taking along a television set so that he wouldn't miss the National League playoffs. That was when they discovered they were in range of none of the many television stations carrying the game.

What all first television set experiences have in common is that they were followed by a common television set experience. The set may have been, in the opinion of the strongest person present, too big and heavy to carry back in the boat. Or it may have sat forgotten in the corner, and have been forgotten again when it came to be time to pack up. Then a new one may have been bought for the home in the city. For whatever reason, the television set stayed.

Around the lakes, television sets stayed, and an industry built up around them. Rooftop antennae were sold and installed; towers were built, tall enough to pull in royal weddings from the most remote points. Publishers in cottage country communities launched giveaway tabloids that featured, along with advertisements for state-of-the-art septic systems, complete television listings. Satellite dishes sprouted from the underbrush, in the places where large water tanks had once been. Unemployed youths found part-time work cutting down large white pines that blocked the air space between the dishes and the satellites. The marina began renting out movies.

The complaining of the old grouches intensified. They complained that there were so many movies for rent at the marina that the selection of plugs, spinners, and leaders had been cut back almost to nothing. But the complaining could no longer be heard over the sounds emanating nightly from the VCRs and the television sets, the music and laughter of movies about young people enjoying the summertime.

The times the old grouches enjoyed the most were the times the power went off. Not that life was easy for them then. While the old grouches had stubbornly resisted electric blankets and clocks, they still had to suffer without food from cans, since the hand-operated can opener had disappeared. Worse, the old grouches had to go without coffee, since coffee could not be ground. Worse still, food could not be cooked, except on a barbecue. And worse than that, they had to make alternative toilet arrangements, because the toilets did not work without the water that did not run without the pump which ran on electricity. And because the outhouse had been torn down.

But the old grouches loved every minute of it. They would talk about how spoiled people were today and what simple pleasures there used to be. They would talk about the pioneers, and how they didn't carry around blends of three different kinds of coffee beans, but would fling ground coffee into a boiling pan of water, or a pan of boiling water. The old grouches would talk about how the pioneers coped quite well without hot water, how they used to wash dishes in streams by pounding them on rocks.

The old grouches were a bit confused on some points. And in fact, there were some cartoons, such as old Huckleberry Hound reruns, to which they were quite attached. But they loved to talk about human progress, and about La Vérendrye and Jacques Cartier and the things they were able to accomplish without even an electric can opener.

Water

That Rock Wasn't There Last Year

There is nothing so important as water. It is recreation, it is sustenance, it is scenery, and the dock would look really silly sitting there surrounded by land. Water is climate, it is refreshment. Water is view. Cottages without a view of the water are hardly cottages at all. Cottages from which it is necessary to drive or bike to get to the water are sneered at by those whose cottages are at water's edge. Water is property value.

With no water there are no water skis, no water moccasins, no water ballet. Which is fine, except that without water there are also no water lilies, no water biscuits, and no water closets. Water matters to cottage people in more ways than you would think.

First, the level of the water matters. If the water is too low, the cottage owner can't get out of his boat and onto a fixed dock without someone helping him up, which makes him feel silly. And he did not come all this way to feel silly. When the water is too low, the boat can't go into the boathouse. Furthermore, the boat keeps bumping into rocks that did not exist before, giving rise to the theory that low water is conducive to the manufacture of large rocks that live at, or just above, propeller level. Though no scientific research has been done on the theory, there is at least superficial evidence to support it. The superficial evidence consists of the number of occurrences of the phrase: "That rock wasn't there last year."

The low water means it is not safe to dive. It means that unneeded objects quietly dropped off the end of the dock in previous years suddenly reappear, just a few feet below the surface, to cries of "What's that, Daddy?" Old metal stairs, vintage soft drink bottles, rusted sunglasses, a diving mask, and a golf ball with "OH SHIT" neatly printed on it all appear, along with what appears to have been part of a bed. The low water means that someone, usually a teen-ager who would sooner be reading *Archie* comics, has to dive in and bring the forgotten treasures to the surface, to be admired and stored where they will take up valuable room. The alternative is for someone older, perhaps his father, to venture into the depths at dusk, when no one is around, and drag the treasures into still deeper water.

Along with the level of the water, the type of water matters too. Most people think there is only one type of water, but water can have many different attributes, and thinking of all of it as H_2O is to oversimplify the situation. Is it fresh or salty, for example. If the lake water is salty, it is probably Great Salt Lake or the Dead Sea, which means that the cottage owner has taken a wrong turn somewhere.

Water can be of the cold or warm type. Some can be too cold to swim in, although not, for some reason, too cold to have cottages on. Lake Superior water, for example, which old-timers remember swimming in during the summer of '55. This does not make northerners any the less likely to brag about Lake Superior, although heaven knows why. Generally speaking, water warm enough to swim in is considered an advantage. So is lack of a distinctive smell. Clarity is nice – though excessive clarity is viewed with suspicion, since it may be a sign of acid rain. While they last, though, it is nice to be able to watch the fish.

Water can be of the weedy type. The presence of weeds, while encouraging to those who regard vegetation as a sign of a healthy lake, is not a selling point. Children are likely to imagine dark, slimy bottom-dwelling creatures hiding in the weeds. Adults are likely to imagine the same thing, but are not willing to admit it, so they say that the weeds make the swimming area look messy, might do harm to the boat's engine, and may help to cause itchy eyes and runny noses.

Water can be of the potable type. Some lakes still have water that people can drink. People who inhabit such lakes are fortunate – a fact they are not reluctant to share with those who inhabit other lakes and buy their water, by the plastic jug-full, from the nearest town. Users of plastic jugs do not hesitate to brag either, their point being that they, unlike those who still pump their drinking water directly from the lake, are not risking gastrointestinal something or other. Such discussions gladden the hearts of plastic jug users and help to compensate for the fact that their drinking water tastes like plastic jugs.

Such discussions, in fact, gladden the hearts of everybody. Which brings to mind another function of water, perhaps the most important: *to be the topic of conversation*.

Friends talk about the water, strangers talk about the water. Even lovers talk about the water . . .

"Is the water cold enough for you, my darling?"

"It tastes like plastic, my love."

When cottage people get together, it is of prime importance that they have something to talk about. If they do not find a topic of conversation close at hand, they will talk about some city thing, such as the stock market, or the absolute necessity of ensuring that there is a sufficient supply of sidewalk cafes without any of them actually operating within earshot of one's house.

Water fills the bill. Is it a bit cooler than usual? Did the algae hold off a bit longer this year? Can you ever remember it being so low? Oh, sure, in '78 it was even lower. No: '78 was the year the weeds were almost gone. The water wasn't all that low.

It is low, though. Have you noticed that new rock just to the south of the marina? Do you think all that foamy stuff is pollution, or is it just soap suds? Well, aren't soap suds pollution? Don't think so: we've always had soap suds. Pollution wasn't invented until the sixties, was it?

There will be a discussion of why the water is so low. Is it the lack of rainfall this summer, or the lack of snowfall the winter before? Are they letting more of it over the dam to make electricity for the city? Or are the Americans taking it? And if they are, why isn't the government doing anything about it?

The dock at any up-to-date cottage is equipped with a water thermometer. The water thermometer is usually read in Fahrenheit, which puzzles children. But it exists only partly to make parents feel superior. It certainly doesn't exist to tell people whether to swim or not; the difference between 72 and 76 is meaningless. The water thermometer exists primarily to enable further conversation. If today it is 72 and yesterday it was 71, that proves something, doesn't it? In fact, it only goes to show what you were always saying.

Yeah, but last week it was 68.

Sure, it was – at *your* place.

What kind of a thermometer do you have?

A better kind than you have.

Oh yeah?

Face it. You just live in a colder part of the lake.

Not a chance. The water at my place has always been warmer. Ever since my father's day.

Easy for you to say. They didn't even have thermometers in those days . . .

Children have been known to steal quietly away from such conversations, using the flimsiest of excuses – such as the need to find proper sticks for roasting marshmallows, even when there are no marshmallows to roast. Some time in the next couple of weeks, the children say, there will be marshmallows to roast and there is nothing like being prepared.

When they grow up, the water will still be there. With any luck, it will have about the same temperature and be about the same colour. But whether it is or not, they will talk about it.

Wilderness

It's a Jungle in There

The wilderness is a state of mind. For some, the wilderness is life without electricity, away from all humanity, in places no one has been before. For other people, the wilderness is a place with only black-and-white TV.

The wilderness can be close or it can be far away. For a small child, the wilderness is behind a bush out of sight of the cottage. He can be a little frightened there, listening to the rustle of trees and things, and knowing, if he wants to think about it, that he can find a parent quickly if necessary. A year or so later, he wants it to be wilder than that. He wants to move to a wilder place, to a spot where he cannot hear his mother talking and his mother cannot hear him.

Being away from cars is enough for some adults in their search for the wilderness, but others can still, when the night is quiet, hear the sound of cars on the distant highway and are bothered by it. Some who cannot hear cars can hear boats, and don't like it. They have to go where it is really wild.

For many, the wilderness is defined by the presence of wild animals. But there is no agreement as to what animals are wild. Mice are wild enough for many. An unclipped dog looks wild to some urbanites. Rabbits are wild animals, just wild enough for some tastes, while others prefer the wildness of garter snakes, which they pick up and try to drop down the back of people's shirts. There is no accounting for taste.

Raccoons seem wild, but so many raccoons are city dwellers now that people venture into the wilderness to get *away* from them. Not that it works. There are tales of raccoons, true tales, fighting their way through screen doors, finding the cupboard, eating up all the Kellogg's Sugar Frosted Flakes and leaving the kitchen in an awful state. Those who want to escape both city and country raccoons are forced farther into the wilderness. They want real wilderness, wild wilderness, where the animals have never seen human beings, have never even seen *movies* of human beings. This means, of necessity, travelling to parts of the lake where human beings have never been.

In most cottage lakes, this is now impossible. Human beings have been just about everywhere. Many is the wilderness fanatic who, at a moment of triumph brought on by not being able to hear the highway, encounters a litter basket. At such times, there is nothing for it but to head farther north.

Remember: *north*. People have tried looking for wilderness in the south, but usually encounter nothing but increasingly citified raccoons, plus traffic heading north.

❋   ❋   ❋

Some go happily into the wilderness, some go merely because it is good for them. Or they think it is good for them. "If I survive," they tell their spouses, "I will be a better person for it." And off they go, muttering to themselves, trying to memorize the things they have studied up on:

Put your food up in a tree.

Put yourself up in a tree if something growls at you, unless it growls from the tree.

Stay away from tall trees in a storm, but remember where they are in case your food is in one of them.

Keep your matches dry.

Look for the north star.

Drown your fires.

Don't panic.

Hang on to the boat.

Liquor just makes you colder, even though it doesn't always feel like it.

Wild animals are more afraid of you than you are of them.

If wild animals do not appear to be more afraid of you than you are of them, running is not such a bad idea.

✳   ✳   ✳

Among the least comfortable wilderness seekers are those who take children along. The idea of this is to expose the children to nature's beauty and power and get them away from *Archie* comics for a few days. If it doesn't cloud over, the northern lights will be there to be seen and there may be a shooting star or two as well. They can fish and eat what they catch, and if they don't catch anything, there is always some powdered stuff and a secret stash of candy bars and potato chips for those sudden intense moments of homesickness for civilization.

As long as the responsible adult does not get frightened, such an expedition can work well. A frightened adult can be bad company – snappish, unreasonable, quick to criticize children for being frightened.

The secret to not being frightened in the wilderness–at least to not being frightened early–is to know where north is. Most adults sneer at this notion and find out – too late! – its significance. The predicament in which they find themselves is a product of the sin of pride. They know where west is, they say. All they have to do is find west and then turn right from it and there they are, looking north.

Which is all very well, except around midday on the first day out, when the sun has not begun to think of setting, some wilderness-seekers experience difficulty. Failing to find west in the sky, they fail to find north. Failing to find north, they fail to read their map. In vain, they look to the map, where north is clearly marked, but find that their place, the place upon which they sit, looking at the map, is not. Or if it is clearly marked, they don't know which clear mark it is.

Expeditions that start well often founder here, with conversations resembling the following:

"Stupid map."

"Why is the map stupid, Daddy?"

"Don't worry. There's nothing to worry about."

"Is there something wrong with the map, Daddy?"

"There's nothing to be afraid of."

"I'm worried, Daddy."

"I know exactly where we are."

"I'm not afraid, Daddy."

"There's nothing to be afraid of."

"I'm afraid."

"Don't be a baby."

"Where are we, Daddy?"

"I'll know in a minute."

"Is a minute up yet?"

"Stop being frightened."

"Is a minute up now, Daddy?"

"I have an idea."

"That's good, Daddy."

"Stop crying and Daddy will tell you what his idea is."

"I'm not crying much now, Daddy."

"Let's stick around here until the sun starts to go down."

"I have an idea, Daddy. Why don't we leave now and head north."

"Well, Daddy thinks it might be easier to do that after the sun goes down."

"But it will be dark then."

"That's true."

"Don't be scared, Daddy."

❋ ❋ ❋

Wilderness trips often end sooner than anticipated. More practical ones involve a journey of fifty yards into the bush. Here can be encountered mosquitoes, garter snakes, toads, and mysterious animal droppings. If the members of the wilderness expedition keep their backs turned to the cottage, they will not be able to see it. If they sing some good wilderness songs, such as "Row, Row, Row Your Boat," they will not hear the black-and-white TV.

And if the adult members of the wilderness expedition are lucky in their choice of younger companions, no one will ask why they are singing a rowing song while walking in the woods.

(The answer, if anyone asks, is: "Keep singing! It frightens away the snakes.")

Part 2

Cottage Man at Work

The Theory
Those Who Work and Those Who Plop in the Chair
The Dock
A Wooden Thing That Often Floats
The Boat
Learning What the Points Are, or Is
The Path
Theology in a Fallen Log
The Deck
Psychology of a Cottage Project
The Present
Less Work, More Noise
The Future
The Septic System Has a Flashing Light

The Theory

Those Who Work and Those Who Plop in the Chair

The first thing Jake does when he gets to the cottage is always the same: he drops his bag on the floor, flops into a chair on the veranda, and says, "Get me a beer, willya? You wouldn't believe the traffic."

When night falls, he will be in the same chair, a number of empty cans will be on the floor beside him, and his bag will still be where he dropped it. When he goes to bed, he will pull a couple of things he needs out of the bag and leave it there. Tomorrow, he will be back in the chair. Bill will be fixing it.

The first thing Bill does when he gets to the cottage is always the same: he puts his bag on the floor, goes to the tool room, and comes back with a hammer, a pry bar, and a shirt pocket full of nails. "I noticed a loose board on the way up," he says. "It'll just take me a minute."

And there goes Bill for the weekend. Bill Jr. wants to tell him about the raccoons, Mrs. Bill wants to tell him about Bill Jr., and Jake wants to talk about the Blue Jays' last home stand. But Bill has found a loose board. While he's fixing the loose board, he will find another loose board, and when he looks under that loose board he will notice the stringer is a little rotten and probably should be replaced.

When dinner has been on the table for half an hour, Bill shows up, still with nails in his pocket, gulps down some food, declines dessert, and asks how late the Beaver Lumber stays open. Then he is off in the boat, leaving Jake to talk about the Blue Jays' last home stand with Mrs. Jake, who would rather not hear about it. When Bill gets back, he carts the lumber up from the dock by himself and begins sawing. It is 9 P.M. Mrs. Bill reminds him about the baby, which Bill remembers easily. He stops sawing, grabs a cup of coffee, and wanders out to the veranda, where Jake is plopped. Jake is out of cigarettes. There are more in his bag, five feet away. He asks Bill to pass him the bag.

"What about those Jays?" Jake says. "You think they can turn it around?"

"The boat sounds funny," Bill answers. "Did you notice that? Just when you slow her down, there's this clunking noise."

❊   ❊   ❊

At every lake, there are men who work and men who plop into the chair. The interesting thing is that the men who plop into the chair think they are working, and the men who work don't know that they are.

Jake always plops into the chair after doing something. He drives from the city, for example. Or he lifts something. Jake is not good at fixing things, or even planning to fix things, but he is good at lifting and carrying. The women, who aren't all that fond of lifting and carrying anyway, have developed the theory that men are born with a primitive need to lift and carry. They call upon Jake from time to time to lift and carry.

Jake will haul himself, sighing, out of his chair, do the appointed task, with grunts, return from it, rubbing his shoulder a little, and plop, sighing, back into the chair. When he returns to the office on Monday, he will tell his colleagues how hard he worked at the cottage. And he will believe it.

Bill's story is somewhat different. Mrs. Bill is always telling Bill to relax. Bill doesn't know what she's talking about. Right now, he's tightening up something in the chair Jake is sitting in. Jake, trying to be helpful, asks if he should get up. Bill says it's not necessary. Jake, sighing, stays in the chair.

Sometimes Jake goes down to the dock where Bill is fixing the boat. "Need any help?" Jake asks.

"Hand me that wrench over there," Bill says. Jake hands him a chisel. Eventually, he finds the wrench. Bill says thanks; Jake says no problem.

If Jake and Bill are brothers and share the same cottage, everything works out fine. The boat runs, the chairs are safe to sit upon, and there is an absence of loose boards. Bill doesn't mind Jake not working because he doesn't really notice him. Jake doesn't feel guilty for not working because he knows he needs his rest. It's when Jake has his own cottage that things get a bit rough. He doesn't know what to carry and he lacks the proper wrenches. When Bill has his own cottage his family is always wanting to go back to the city, so that they can spend some time with him.

The Dock

A Wooden Thing That Often Floats

Real or imagined, work is a part of cottage life. For some it is
the biggest part; for others it is a necessary evil. The Protestant
ethic lurks beneath the skin of even those who are neither
Protestant nor ethical: (a) you work; (b) you play. It is the
proportion of (a) to (b) that marks the differences between
people. For all of them, at the cottage there are things to do.
The things to do can be divided into traditional things and
newfangled things. The list of traditional things begins with the
dock.

The dock is important for many reasons. It is the first thing
people see when they come to the cottage, so it creates an
impression. The dock is the thing people sit on to read books,
lie upon to get a suntan. They cast fishing lures from it. They
tie up boats to it. They have lunch on it. They work on it. And
they work on it.

Many bad things can happen when a dock is not well looked
after. Children can fall through rotten boards and scrape their
knees. When, after three hours, they are still complaining about
their knee hurting, even though Mercurochrome and Band-
Aids have been applied, they will have to be taken to the doctor.
This means finding the doctor, who may be plopped in a chair

having his fourth gin and tonic and talking about the Jays' last home stand. Or it may mean going to the local clinic, where the nurse looks at the child's knee and decides that it will be seen after the bee sting on the elbow, the fish hook in the thumb, the swimmer's ear, and the funny-looking bump on the left shin the mother knows is silly to worry about but she just can't help it.

The most horrible thing a poorly maintained dock can do is float away. This does not happen very often, but it is always embarrassing when it does. Floating docks secured to the land, or to permanent docks, by ropes and chains sometimes break loose. When they do so, they always head for places where they can cause the greatest humiliation to their owners. The marina, for example, is a bad place for your floating dock to float to.

When you come searching for your dock, people are there, at the marina, some of them wise in the ways of the lake, some of them quick with a quip.

"I was *wondering* whose that was," one will say, as you coast in, trying to appear casual. Then they will fall to reminiscing about great dock floats of years gone by. To demonstrate that you are a good sport, you will have to stay there the whole time, chuckling appreciatively every few minutes. Some of these people who are wise in the ways of the lake can be quite deliberate in their telling of a story.

Worse yet, they will offer to help. Just as you try to make your way back to the cottage, as unobtrusively as a man can with a 15-by-8-foot dock tied to his outboard, they will all leap up and begin shouting directions to each other about your dock and where it should be tied and whether she is floating too high at the bow or too low at the stern. A larger crowd will gather, and you will hear mutterings at the fringes of it as the newcomers arrive.

"What's going on?" a voice will say.

"Fella's dock floated away," will come the answer. "Guess he didn't have it tied right."

Too late, as you make your way slowly out of the bay,

waving cheerily at the crowd at the marina, you will remember
muskrats. Muskrats eat holes in ropes. That's what happened.
Muskrats chewed holes in the ropes holding your dock. Nothing
you could do about it.

But it's too late to turn around. Besides, you're not sure
the boat *will* turn around, with a floating dock tied behind it.

Still, there are worse places for your dock to end up. An
Anglican bishop's dock worked its way loose in a high wind
one night. The next day dawned sunny and clear, a beautiful
day, only the dock was gone. The bishop cursed (after making
sure no one was looking), and set out in his ancient 9.5-horse-
power Johnson to find it. He found it in the middle of the
regatta. Skilful sailors were sailing around it. Less skilful sailors
were sailing into it.

As the bishop arrived on the scene, official-looking boats
were circling his rogue dock and men in blazers were talking to
each other on ship-to-shore telephones and calling out to the
sailboats with loud-hailers.

"Attention! Attention! There is a floating dock in the middle of the course. Please be careful! Repeat: There is a floating
dock in the middle of the course. Please be careful!"

The message was then repeated in French.

You, upon sizing up the situation, would have turned
around and headed home, leaving the sailboats to fend for
themselves, and hoping that the dock would return of its own
volition under cover of darkness. Or you would have blundered
into the middle of it all, making woeful apologies that would
have been relayed over the loud-speaker system to the entire
fleet.

"Attention! Attention! The owner of the floating dock is
here. Repeat: The owner of the floating dock is here, the one
that has caused such a disturbance in the regatta. He says he
can't understand how it got away and will have it out of the
course shortly. Repeat: He says he can't understand how it got
away and will have it out of the course shortly. Thank you for

your patience. In the meantime, please be careful. Repeat: Please be careful!"

But nothing like that could happen to a bishop. Wearing civilian clothes – he had considered briefly whether a show of the purple would be helpful, then decided against it – he coasted to the floating dock and jumped out on it, tying up his boat and declaiming in the manner of a dotty Englishman.

"Frightful bother," he bellowed, to no one in particular. "One never knows where one's dock will fetch up these days," adding, "Here, mind your spinnaker" as a sailboat narrowly missed running into the dock.

"Quite a bit of a breeze last night. And muskrats, you know. Nibble nibble nibble. Heh-heh. One's dock floating all over tarnation. Terrible situation. How's the race? Looks quite stunning from over there," he said, pointing in the direction from which he had not come, then started up his outboard with one pull and set off, scattering sailboats in his wake and waving to the captains and crew.

Such tales are told when losers of floating docks gather around the live bait tank at the marina. There is always an argument as to whether it is worse to have the dock float in to the marina or to have it turn up in the middle of the regatta. Each has its advocates. And there is a third school of thought – that the worst thing to have happen when a dock floats away is not to know where it is at all.

This always happens to a tidy person, a person so neat in his personal habits, so organized in his treatment of his possessions, so regular in his habits that he is invariably resented by the very people who always elect him secretary-treasurer of every organization to which he belongs.

The dock gets away. It is not in the middle of the regatta. It has not drifted into another bay on his property or his neighbours'. It has not floated in to the marina. It is nowhere in sight. The tidy person knows instantly where to find his German binoculars, and he knows instantly the best vantage point on his property from which to scan the entire lake. He takes the binoculars to the highest point, sweeps the lake with his accountant's eye, and finds nothing.

Then he has to begin a serious search. Stepping carefully into his finely tuned boat, the spark plugs clean, the points adjusted, the proper number of paddles, life preservers and flotation cushions on board, the tidy person sets out. At each dock he must tie up and alight. Only then does his customary precision of speech desert him.

"You wouldn't happen to have seen a – well, a – sort of a, kind of dock sort of thing around here, would you? Mine seems to be – well, it will, I know it will turn up and it's probably silly of me even to – well, must be going, thanks for your help, bye."

Mischievous neighbours will ask the tidy person to *describe* the dock, which he, lacking any notion of irony, is quite capable of doing. "It's a wooden thing," he will begin.

❋   ❋   ❋

The dock has always been a wooden thing, but it has evolved over the years, developing modern twists and regional variations. The old dock didn't float. It sat on cribs: logs spiked together into crude boxes into which were dumped large rocks. This gave the foundation weight and stability and kept it from being moved about by the ice in winter.

The first floating docks came into being at about the same time that serious sun-tanning hit North America. The old dock with cribs was nice and solid and good for tying boats to, but it lacked sun-tanning space. The people who built the old dock with the cribs had vivid memories of doing so and were damned if they were going to build another one. That was for the next generation. So a compromise was reached: an extension would be added to the dock. The extension would have no cribs. It would just float.

Early floating docks did not float very well, at least not for long. In time, and not much of it, they began sinking. Bays all over North America are still littered with the half-floating remains of floating docks.

Various other methods were tried. Big oil drums full of air. Styrofoam logs. These worked fairly well in the west, but were found by Central Ontario cottage owners to be ideal muskrat food. Some owners put styrofoam inside inner tubes. Others found giant plastic mustard vats and tried to strap docks to them. Some went so far as to consider cribs of logs filled with stones.

No matter how well the dock works, there is always work to be done on it. Boats bang into the dock. Children run on it. Heavy things are dropped on it. One corner sags. Two corners sag. One hinge is almost out. One of the chains is getting rusty. It is floating too low. It is floating too high. The older people are having trouble getting out of the boat.

A work-oriented person can spend his entire three weeks without ever leaving the dock, except to eat. And if he is lucky with the weather, he can eat there too.

The Boat

Learning What the Points Are, or Is

Whether used for pleasure or for work, the boat is a source of constant worry and the subject of constant conversation. If all else fails, if the weather has been the same for five days in a row, if no strange sounds have been heard in the bush overnight, if no one has heard the morning news on a transistor radio – then "How's the boat running these days?" will always work as a conversation-starter.

"The boat" means "the boat with the motor in it." Other boats are less bother and need not be conversed about. A canoe always goes. It may leak, but if you can find a paddle or two, it is no problem. A rowboat always goes. The oarlocks may squeak, one oar may be missing, and you may have to stand up and paddle it like an inefficient gondolier, which takes some of the romance out of it, if that's what you had in mind. Still, one way or another, the rowboat goes.

The motorboat may not. Motorboats can do more things now than they ever could before. They can go fast. They can plane. They can honk their horns. They can make music in AM or FM. They can find fish. They can bail themselves. They can telephone the shore. Boats can do almost anything cars can do.

And like cars, the more things they can do, the more things they can stop doing when something goes wrong.

When something goes wrong with a great big expensive boat with built-in bar, AM-FM tape deck with 12-band equalizer, cruise control, and a Confederate flag flying from the stern, there is not much to do but take it to the shop, particularly if what has gone wrong has to do with the engine. The engine is down below everything and the owners can't get at it. Not that they'd want to.

However, a certain amount of maintenance can be done at the dock. This consists mainly of polishing and buffing and looking for marks. Rowboats and little outboard motors are always bumping against big expensive boats at marinas and the docks of waterfront supermarkets. Inevitably these collisions leave marks, which the big boat owners can fret about, scour off, polish and buff before settling down to relax for the rest of the day.

Smaller, less expensive boats have the disadvantage that their motors are out in the open, almost inviting tampering and tinkering. You can lift the motor out of the water and look at the propeller. You can take the motor right off the boat and lay it down on the dock so you can walk around it and say it looks all right to you. You can tighten this and loosen that. You can cause oil and grease to spill out all over the dock so that people who want to sunbathe complain about you and your filthy old boat. With a lot of new things, including cars, the manufacturer is always warning you not to tamper, not to take off the cover that is there for your own protection. In new appliances and new cars, parts are sealed and never need maintenance. But not so with outboard motors.

Over the years a few new things have gone wrong with outboard motors. Most of these have to do with the starter. When you can start an engine just by pushing a button, instead of pulling a rope the way you're supposed to, more things can go wrong. And the kinds of things that go wrong tend to be electrical, capable of being fixed only at the marina. Such things tend to be expensive. Or it could simply be a case of the battery being shot, which tends to be expensive. This is why most people prefer to start by looking for loose connections.

The possibility of loose connections is one of the two things every person understands about electricity. The other is short circuits, and nobody understands them really all that well, aside from not wanting to be personally involved in one. The way to test for loose connections is to disengage all the wires that were previously engaged to each other. This is done with a screwdriver. Then engage them all again. If the push-button starter works, then there was a loose connection. If the push-button starter doesn't work and there are sparks and a funny smell, then there may or may not have been a loose connection but it is impossible to tell because the way they have been reconnected is not the way they were connected originally.

Often neither of these two things happens. Instead, the disconnector of the wires is called away to do something else, like have a glass of lemonade, and when he comes back he realizes that he has sort of – well, it's not exactly that he's *forgotten* where the wires went, but he doesn't want to take unnecessary chances about it, because of the children and so on. Some discussion inevitably follows and just as inevitably the engine and its push-button starter wind up at the marina, waiting for the guy to fix it.

All of this happens because electricity is such a mystery to most people. They see that it comes out of little holes in the wall and they don't understand how, and so they decide not to mess with it. Your basic outboard motor with the rope that starts it is in a different category. Generations of Canadians have grown up with it, and each knows that there are only four things that can be wrong with it:

1. The prop hit a log and broke a shear pin.
2. The mixture.
3. Dirty gas.
4. The points.

The shear pin is supposed to keep the bottom of the engine from falling off. When the propeller hits a rock or a log or someone's wayward floating dock, the shear pin breaks and the engine makes a horrible sound. Proper procedure then is to haul up the engine and begin looking under the seats for new shear pins. Under the seats are old empty oil cans, half-empty tubes of insect repellent, the screwdriver you've been looking for since last summer, and twenty-seven cents. Upon discovering all this, proper procedure is to stand up in the boat and scratch your head until someone comes along and offers you a tow to the marina. You do not admit to them that you hit the bishop's floating dock and you don't have an extra shear pin. You say it must be the points.

No one knows what the points are, or is. People pretend to. A typical scene involving points has several men huddling around a disassembled engine and muttering. One or two of them – usually those with post-graduate degrees – spit into the water. A little boy comes up and says: "Why won't the engine go, Daddy?" Daddy says: "It's the points, Tommy."

Then comes the key moment, the one that literally separates the men from the boys. Tommy says: "What are the points, Daddy?"

Daddy replies: "It's kind of hard to explain," and Tommy runs off to find something more interesting to do.

In some parts of the country, men are more likely to talk about the gap than the points, but it is more or less the same thing. They put the motor back together and sometimes it runs and sometimes it doesn't. Then they take it to the marina.

Problems with the mixture usually occur while the boat is running and a sudden change in the pitch of the engine is detected. This gives the men the opportunity to fiddle with the knobs marked "HIGH SPEED" and "LOW SPEED" on the engine. Often such work is delegated to the youngsters, since little real harm can come of it and it gives them a gentle introduction into the world of engine maintenance. If the boat still sounds funny, then blame can be laid at the feet of the kid at the marina who filled the tanks and was too busy chatting up the girls to pay attention to how much oil he was mixing in with the gas.

This, the inattentive kid whose looks you don't like at the gas pump at the marina, is also a probable cause of the fourth common outboard engine problem – dirty gas. (A regional variation is "water in the gas.")

Dirty gas has the same symptoms as other common ailments –namely, that the engine sounds funny. But it has the advantage of no one having to do anything about fixing it. The dirty gas is, to be sure, clogging up various things inside the engine, but no permanent harm is done, and once it's used up the engine will be all right again.

It is sometimes observed that people who enjoy tinkering with engines run into a lot of problems with the points, while people who don't are more frequently troubled by dirty gas.

The Path

Theology in a Fallen Log

The path around the cottage can take many turns. Some paths are gaily decorated. Little wooden animals and elves of various nationalities peep out of the woods. White benches are located at strategic places, painted annually and dusted daily. The path itself, wide enough to drive a truck over, and free of all but the most decorative stones, is covered with the kind of wood chips available in garden stores.

It is commonly thought that such paths mark the cottage properties of little old ladies, but this is not so. Cottagers of all ages and sexes fit the description of those who would tame the wilderness, decorate it suitably, and turn it into something that resembles, more than anything else, a miniature golf course.

Once such a habitat has been established, it requires remarkably little maintenance. The largest trees have already been taken down, to prevent their falling on plaster geese, and the brush has been cut way back, to prevent real animals from interfering, in any way, with store-bought ones. Only a bit of snipping and clipping is needed to keep the paths free of anything that might scratch or dirty a user.

Certainly, there is nothing for a woodsman to do–a woodsman being defined as a man on vacation with a plaid shirt on his back and an axe in his hand. And, of course, a woodsman wouldn't go within miles of the place. Snipping and clipping and dusting white benches are not enough for him. His work is with the axe and the saw. It is how he proves himself. Even if he is not so great with motors, even if he is a bit vague about the finer points of the points, his spirits soar when it is time to clear the path.

No one can mess up clearing the path. There are no small metal objects to turn, no little screws that you can't remember where they went. Just trees and limbs and bushes, waiting to be chopped, sawn, and tossed deeper into the woods. The path clearer's mistakes will not be seen, only the path. It is for this reason that doctors often make good path clearers.

The path could go just about anywhere. It may be a path around the main house; it may lead to the water, to the out-house, or to the place where the outhouse used to be; it may lead to the road or to the other side of the island. No matter where it goes, it is a path and it needs work.

In path clearing, as in other forms of cottage work, certain philosophical questions arise. These have to do with how clear the path should be. No, actually they have to do with something far more fundamental than that – they have to do with how clear *God* would want the path to be. And whether that is clear enough.

This is not one of those philosophical cottage questions in which men naturally fall on one side and women on the other. The Path Question revolves not so much on differences between the sexes as on attitudes to neatness, or attitudes to nature. In addition, the sub-theme of laziness lies just beneath the surface. The main consideration, however, is theological.

Let's follow Hank and Sheila as they walk the path for the first time this summer. They stoop to pick up small branches. They climb over a spruce that has fallen across the path, and Hank speaks.

"We'll have to come back and get that one," he says.

Sheila is not so sure. "I guess. But it looks sort of neat,

lying across the path like that. It makes the path look kind of, I don't know, wild and unspoiled."

"Unspoiled or not," Hank replies, "somebody's going to trip over it."

Sheila gazes up into the arch of trees overhead. "You know," she says, "probably that's the way things used to be. A tree would fall and it would just lie there and become part of the scenery until millions of years later, or maybe thousands, it would become soil. Then another tree would fall . . ."

"Let's get out of here before another tree falls," Hank says.

The discussion continues. God meant the tree to fall, is Sheila's main point, and who are she and Hank to interfere with His plan. Hank doubts God meant the tree to fall at all. It was probably an accident. Who knows, they could be doing God a *favour* by cutting up the spruce tree, making it into firewood and dragging the rest of it out of sight into the woods.

Depending upon what mood they are in, the discussion can take several turns, one of which turns it into an argument.

"I don't know why you always want this place to look like a damn country club," Sheila yells. "Isn't Nature good enough for you?"

"This isn't Nature," Hank roars back. "This is a goddamn mess!"

If you get Hank in a quieter moment, he will say that he likes Nature well enough, but that Nature has some things that don't make sense, like poison ivy right on the little path to the kids' treehouse. Nature has swamps and swamps have mosquitoes. Nature has roots where you can trip over them. Nature has weeds all over the nice sandy beach. There's no reason, Hank figures, why nature can't be improved on at least a little bit. Sure, God made the poplar tree. But didn't God also have a bit of a hand in making the chain saw?

The argument about poplar trees and chain saws has been going on for about as long as Hank and Sheila have had this place. It is Hank's belief that one was made for the other. Sheila, theological as ever, is of the opinion that the poplar tree was put on earth for some grander reason. This provokes another discussion.

"The wood doesn't burn worth a damn," Hank says, "and the stupid things are always dying and falling on people's houses. We should just cut them all down before they get big enough to hurt somebody."

Sheila has a difficult time, as most defenders of trees do, matching him logical argument for logical argument. "I think they're beautiful," she says, in desperation.

"I think they're useless," Hank replies. "If they were put here for a reason, how come the beavers are always cutting them down?"

"That's a good reason," Sheila says, perhaps a bit tentatively. "Beavers need things to eat."

"Sure," Hank says. "But you think they would have put them a little closer to the ground."

"You know what we'll get if we cut down all the poplar trees," Sheila says.

"What?" asks Hank.

"Lazy beavers."

In the end, the argument over the spruce across the path resolves itself. Every time Hank has to step over it, he makes a mental note to bring the saw with him the next time. Every next time he forgets to bring the saw. The spruce stays. Next summer, when Hank goes to saw it up, the kids protest. They say it's always been there. It's a part of the cottage tradition.

In ten years, the spruce will rot away and Hank will notice, when he opens the cottage, that there is no tree across the path. He will quietly, without telling anybody, drop one, in about the same spot. Sheila will notice that it's a poplar, and perhaps the older kids will too, but no one will say anything about it.

The Deck

Psychology of a Cottage Project

In the city, there are people who like meetings. Most people are not like that. For most people, meetings are an interruption. Meetings get in the way of useful work. Meetings are a pain in the neck, to be avoided at best, endured at worst, and ended as soon as possible.

But some people look forward to meetings. They spend their time planning for meetings. The meeting is the highlight of their day. For such people, the best possible decision taken at a meeting is the one that leads to further meetings.

Frustration would seem to await a meeting-oriented person at the cottage. In a small, single-family group, meetings are not rewarding. The subject matter – for example, the question of picking up one's dirty socks – lacks weight, and may in fact be identical to that of family meetings held from time to time over the fall and winter months. No one wants to pack up the car and drive all the way to the cottage just to have the same family meetings that took place in the city in November.

Even in larger, multi-family groups, the subject matter is not, as they say in the city, meeting-susceptible. Few worthwhile meetings have been held about trees, for example. The only decision that can be taken about a tree is whether it will live or

die. Many urban options are simply not available in such primitive surroundings: the tree cannot be moved; there is little point
in painting it; and while the option of studying it further is
always available, it is somehow unsatisfying.

Anyway, there is an unspoken consensus that inhibits discussion: live trees are allowed to continue living; dead trees are
already dead. The only decision left to be made is whether the
dead ones should be cut down or allowed to fall down. While
interesting things can be said pro or con on such a subject, the
discussion is not likely to last long – certainly not long enough
for a true meeting fanatic.

Although there is limited scope for meetings at the cottage,
they do occur, but not around a table. Instead, they shift to the
site of whatever project is on for that day. Before any actual
work – any cutting, digging, chopping, sawing, or nailing – can
take place, it is necessary to discuss. Such discussions are not
called meetings. They are called discussing the project. But they
are meetings.

Typically, discussions of the project take place after the
project has been agreed upon in principle. Then, and only then,
after the workforce and the tools have been assembled at the
site, will the first serious consideration of alternatives take place.

Let's put a name to the project. Call it a deck. It has been
agreed, somehow, that the deck will be square and that it will
sit just down from the main house, overlooking the dock. A
sketch has been made, the lumber has been purchased and sits
there waiting. Four men and two boys, all vaguely related, some
by marriage, assemble. The boys would sooner be engaged in a
typical summertime leisure activity, such as reading *Archie*
comics, but their fathers have decided that it is time for them
to move along the path to manhood by becoming involved in
some serious work. The boys are seven and six, respectively.

There are no women present, for various reasons. Perhaps
the most relevant is that they know a discussion is going to take
place. They know the discussion is going to take more than an
hour and while that discussion is taking place, no work is going

to be done. Women hate discussions. They would sooner work. In the city, women are lousy in meetings, because they insist on the meetings coming to a decision quickly and adjourning, leaving the men with nothing to do for the rest of the day.

There is no chairman, as such, when the discussions begin, but one of the men will always act in that capacity. He will be easy to recognize because he has a metal tape measure clipped to his belt. (Some men, perhaps less confident in their leadership abilities, will carry a level; others will tie a carpenter's apron full of nails about their waists. But the tape measure is the *sine qua non* of cottage discussion leaders.)

While there are some members of the crew who are content to nail and saw where they are told to nail and saw, there are always those who lust for the power and prestige of the discussion leader's role. In one known case, five members of the same crew all turned up wearing tape measures. Immediate tension was apparent, but eventually resolved without incident when it was discovered that two did not have pencils, one wore his tape measure inside-out, and a fourth was wearing penny loafers.

It is the Discussion Leader's role to defend the original concept of the project. He may allow discussion to range over a wide variety of alternatives, up to and including the triple-decker deck with the firemen's pole down the middle for the kids to have fun with, but in the end the discussion leader must ensure that the final project bears some resemblance to what he has on the piece of paper he carries in his shirt pocket.

Discussion Leaders always have, in addition to tape measures, shirt pockets.

Discussion usually begins when one of the crew – call him the Initiator – notices some hitherto unrecognized feature of the site, a rock outcropping, perhaps, or a large root. It begins innocuously enough.

"I wonder if we can get it over this baby here," the Initiator says, using the established terminology. On a project, any object, be it a rock, a root, a tree, or a steep cliff, is always referred to as "this baby."

This leads to a mini-discussion, followed by sightings along pieces of string, several placements of the level, and even a quiet, although somewhat theatrical use of the tape measure by the Discussion Leader.

A good Discussion Leader keeps the meaning of his measurements cryptic as long as he can. "Thirty-three point six," he might say, sheathing his tape measure and reaffixing it to his belt.

"It might be a little high," he will say, without bothering to explain what thirty-three point six had to do with anything.

Discussion can now begin, accompanied by various pencil sketches on lumber. In the case of the root – a.k.a. "this baby" – being too high, various alternatives are presented:

1. The root will need to be cut out with an axe. Discussion of this alternative – the quickest, easiest, and most logical one – is carried on in hushed tones, because the men know what it means. The tree will die. Several of the women, as well as some of the children, are known to object to any tree dying before its time. They must not hear the discussion. The two boys, whose loyalties are still questionable, are sent to find screwdrivers.

2. The whole deck can sit higher, with the root staying and the end opposite it being built up. This might make it difficult for the older people – that is, those who are older than the men working on the project – to get up and down. It will also necessitate a recalculation of the stair heights and depths – the rise and run, as somebody claims it is called.

3. The deck could be made smaller, an alternative rejected by the boys when they return with the screwdrivers.

4. The deck could retain its planned shape but be moved three feet to the south. There will be some discussion as to whether it is south or southwest. One of the men grew up always thinking of that way as the south; another grew up thinking of it as the southwest. Apparently their fathers never compared notes on directions. A further point is that the deck, if it were moved three feet south or southwest, would cover just the tiniest bit of the vegetable garden Aunt Edith started

twenty-five years ago that produced a tomato in 1978. As luck would have it, Aunt Edith is on the premises at the moment and has given indications that she remembers the garden.

5. The deck could become smaller, avoiding both the root and the vegetable garden, but it could have a second level built on it, and perhaps a third. With a fireman's pole down the middle for the kids to slide down. The boys seem excited by this idea and are sent off to find more screwdrivers. When they return they will be told to knock off for the day and the men will break for lunch.

The Present

Less Work, More Noise

People like to think they are returning to the old days when they go to the cottage. They also prefer an air-conditioned car in which to return to the old days. Somehow, they are surprised when they get there. They climb out of the air-conditioned car, the little voice in the dashboard reminding them to turn off the lights – and they find the old days are nowhere to be found.

Finding the old days missing, today's cottagers look for something to blame. Here it is. Two things have taken the old days away: electricity and the chain saw. Not much good can be said for either of them.

Before electricity, cottages needed wood. The wood they needed served far more than its present purpose, which is to look pretty in the fireplace. Wood was to cook with. No wood, no cook.

Gathering wood and making it suitable to cook with was a time-consuming and labour-intensive activity. That is, it gave everybody something to do. Wood had to be found, sawed into logs, dragged back to the cottage, sawed into stove lengths, and chopped into firewood.

The sawing was the time-consuming part. Two people on a cross-cut saw could take hours making stove lengths out of a dozen logs, all the while hoping that they would get a turn at chopping, which was the woodpile's version of a glamour profession. A morning's work on the woodpile might involve five or six people. There was sun, sawdust, companionship, and, by lunch time, a feeling that a day's work had been done, and a half-day's loafing on the dock was more than deserved.

The chain saw changed all that. With a chain saw, one person could do the work of six. Without anything to do, the other five could sit around and watch, inhaling gasoline fumes and having their future powers of hearing diminished. Or they could go into the cottage and read *Archie* comics. Later on in the day, when it came to be *time* to read *Archie* comics, the potential readers would lack the sense of accomplishment that would allow them to enjoy reading *Archie* comics. Plus, they would have read them already.

With the chain saw, work, which had once been something everybody had to do every day, became something that one or two people might do in a noisy burst, once every couple of weeks.

The result should not be underestimated. A spirit of teamwork is necesary to make any cottage run, and a spirit of teamwork leads to a spirit of companionship. Companionship develops on the woodpile, in such things as laughing when somebody's aunt gets a log dropped on her foot. Without companionship, the combination of paranoia and claustrophobia we have come to know as cottage fever can develop. When cottage fever hits, bits of jigsaw puzzles are thrown into the forest for no reason and key pages are secretly torn out of old adventures of The Saint. Cottage Man's very survival is threatened. Because of this, it is necessary that work be done and done together.

There is an important additional factor to take into account. Guilt. Many people who have cottages feel guilty about having them. They are conscious of others who do not have cottages or are stuck in traffic. Guilt keeps Cottage Man from enjoying himself. Guilt prevents him from paying sufficient attention to the latest Benny Cooperman mystery while lying in a hammock in the shade. Guilt can only be prevented by work. The labour-saving chain saw creates not only guilt but sore backs as well, plus a terrible vibration in the hands, leading to the fear of never being able to play the violin again, even for those who never could.

Electricity, while usually quieter than a chain saw, has worse effects. Electricity eliminates even the work that the chain saw had to do. With electricity, Cottage Man – or, to be truthful, Cottage Woman – cooks at the flip of a switch. Wood need be chopped and sawed only for decorative purposes. Guilt mounts. The electric cottager is forced to invent things to do, so as to earn his suntan. He must paint things. He must rearrange the tools in the tool shed. If he does not have a tool shed, he must build one. If he lacks the tools to build a proper tool shed, he must buy them. Meanwhile, he must create a temporary storage area for his new tools while he builds the tool shed.

It is because of electricity that the landscape is cluttered by so many temporary tool sheds around the lakes.

But electricity, while it changes the nature of Cottage Man's work, cannot change his *need* to work. There is work to do in the kitchen, of course – the same amount of work that there always was, with the exception of it not being necessary to throw wood on the stove. But Cottage Man refuses to go into the kitchen, except to get a drink of water and use SNAP to wash the grease off his hands. He is in the wilderness, where men go to be men and there is no precedent for kitchens.

Not all men must work. There is Jake, who is down at the dock, having persuaded someone to carry his chair down there. Jake is happy about electricity, because it produces ice cubes. But most men need to feel they have worked, even if they haven't accomplished anything other than rearranging the tools.

There is the boathouse. Things could be rearranged in there. Some of those things could be thrown away. But the modern way of throwing things away is unsatisfying somehow. It lacks the sense of adventure of the old way, which was to put things in the boat, take them out to the middle of the lake in the middle of the night and drop them over the side. Now the things to be thrown away must be placed in green garbage bags and taken to the proper place, where there is probably a store nearby, which several of the children need to visit in order to buy frozen slurpy things that stick to the boat, as well as new *Archie* comics.

The new way, while it may be unpleasant enough to qualify as work, is not work – in the sense we know work. That is, it does not leave a person covered in sawdust. Cottage Man can get no satisfaction from it. His guilt remains, his skin goes untanned. He is unfulfilled. He has brought his family into the wilderness – true, the highway is four lanes now – and there is no work for him to do. His family is provided for without his having provided it. Saddened, without knowing why, Cottage Man putters about, testing the fuses, oiling the chain saw, and arranging things on the shelves of the tool house.

The Future

The Septic System Has a Flashing Light

As he presses on into the future and looks for meaningful work, Cottage Man finds fewer and fewer things he can fix. This is a regrettable development, since fixing things has been a constant in the cottage work ethic over the years. Sometimes fixing things was hard work, sometimes it was undertaken in place of hard work. Whichever way, there were always things to fix, and at least the illusion that they were fixable.

That is less so now, and it will be even less so in the future. The things that break are complicated, electronic, newfangled gadgets. They exist not to be worked on but to be worried about and paid for. In the future, cottage work will be for highly trained specialists.

Already, the shape of the future presents itself around the lake. The shape of the future is the satellite dish. It is the state-of-the-art septic system.

The satellite dish exists to keep people from reading. More properly, it exists to keep people from reading anything other than the satellite TV guide, which lists 975 stations. Figuring out which of 975 programs to watch (although many are repeats) can keep people out of trouble, the water, and the sun for an entire summer. Defenders of satellite dishes say television reception is terrible at the cottage. When asked why they need television reception at all, defenders of satellite dishes look at you like you are crazy.

When the satellite dish needs adjustment – for example, if it is pointed at the Big Dipper instead of at the appropriate communications satellite – Cottage Man seizes the opportunity to perform meaningful labour. He does this by turning the satellite dish this way and that, a project involving at least four people: two to turn the dish, one to watch the 975 channels, and one to yell out the window. If turning it does not work, defenders of satellite dishes are quite prepared to cut down whatever tree stands between the cottage family and a sharper TV image.

The satellite dish must also be painted and polished. Defenders of satellite dishes recognize that there is no point in having a satellite dish at the cottage unless everyone can see that they have it. Providing maximum visibility for the satellite dish may also require the thinning of trees and underbrush blocking the view of the dish enjoyed by those passing by on the lake.

The proper functioning of the state-of-the-art septic system is, to some cottagers, even more important than having 975 functioning television channels. There is no accounting for taste.

Like the satellite dish, the state-of-the-art septic system defies understanding. Unlike the satellite dish, the state-of-the-art septic system has few people who are actually all that eager to understand it.

They understood its predecessor. Its predecessor was a hole in the ground. Before the hole in the ground was the ground. After the hole in the ground was a small house built over the hole in the ground. Little maintenance was required. Usually, something to read would be left in the house. An air freshener would be installed. At the beginning of the season, the cobwebs would be dusted off the house. At the end of the season some sawdust would be dumped down the hole, or some lye, to speed decomposition. Some cottagers would put a fish down the hole, for reasons that were not always easy to explain.

After a year or two, the house would be moved to a new hole, in one of the trickier and most perilous manoeuvres in cottagedom, given that before it could be moved to a new hole it had to be moved off the old one.

For many decades, there were few complaints about such a septic arrangement. It was neither cosy nor warm, but it had a nice view of the woods, if you left the door open, and besides, what was the alternative? The alternative was the woods.

When opposition developed, it was two-pronged. The Environment Police decided that the septic arrangement did not meet Certain Standards. And the new breed of cottager decided that more comfort was needed in septic arrangements. Real bathrooms were installed, with real sinks and toilet seats.

This was nice, but real bathrooms needed something more refined underneath them than a hole in the ground and something more sanitary than a pipe leading into the lake. Mankind's leading thinkers have been devoting their energies to this problem for many years, with a notable lack of success.

What they have come up with so far is an extremely expensive contraption that almost does a number of quite incredible things with sewage and has lights that go on to alert the Lucky Owner of any possible trouble, such as the extremely expensive contraption not working. Ideally, the extremely expensive contraption should be able to make the sewage do everything short of singing and dancing–this being based on the assumption that nobody really wants singing and dancing sewage–but so far, the most reliable part of it is the light that says it is not working. The light rarely fails.

It may be that the extremely expensive contraption is being asked to do too much. A recent version takes the sewage and puts it into a tank, then tries to force the sewage to stir itself up and make bubbles, while at the same time ceasing to be smelly and pumping itself up a hill, there to rest quietly, never bothering anybody again.

The inevitable failure of such a system, and all systems like it, is probably the result of sewage not being smart enough to accomplish all the things demanded of it. Inevitably, the system breaks down, its temporary incapacitation signalled by one of the reliable lights on the control panel. The Lucky Owner, no matter how great his passion for work, suddenly finds himself wanted at the other side of the property, or even back at the office, should it be within easy driving distance.

Among the many problems associated with the extremely expensive contraption is that it cannot easily be taken to the shop. So a repair person must be summoned, a repair person who is very busy all over the lake, dealing with other sewage that also refuses to do tricks. When he arrives, he offers helpful advice, such as: Don't flush the toilet. The Lucky Owner, if he happens to be around when repairs are being made, makes a point of not learning how to do them. When subsequent breakdowns occur, he is quick to blame them on an electronic malfunction. He is helpless again.

In the face of modern technology and modern helplessness, Cottage Man asserts his manhood in the only way left open to him. He spends money. He buys gadgets, the latest gadgets, toys that will, in the fullness of time, gather dust in the boathouse, be placed in green garbage bags and be taken to the dump. For a brief period, however, Cottage Man will become a front-line soldier in man's continuous fight against solitude, beauty, and silence.

The gas-powered water ski will be first, followed by the solar-powered canoe with its own stereo system, followed by the propane-driven pasta maker and the one-person helicopter ("see nature the way it's meant to be seen"). There will be new sailboats, motorboats with bigger motors, and a state-of-the-art septic system capable of being monitored, by means of closed-circuit television and a system of red and green flashing lights, from the master bedroom. There will be an electric fireplace with realistic-looking wood. There will be a dishwasher, to show that Cottage Man can still provide for his woman, and – inevitably – large-screen TV. Soon, thanks to guilt, electricity, and man's urge to progress, the cottage will be just like home.

Part 3

The Ages of Cottage Man

The Early Years
Dark Things in Dark Places
The Teen Years
A Sudden Lack of Interest in Toads
The Parental Years
Life with Dragons
The Later Years
The Pressure on Grandpa

The Early Years

Dark Things in Dark Places

The water is deep and dark underneath and there are great, big slimy things near the bottom. Sometimes they swim up to the surface and grab little kids. You never actually saw that happen, but you've heard things from your friends and your older cousins. They are down there all right.

Still, your parents are insisting that you swim. You can't believe it, given the big slimy things, but there it is. For quite a few years, at least as long as you can remember, you've been quite satisfied with the inflatable turtle. A couple of armbands to keep you afloat, the inflatable turtle to lie on, and you could kick your way around the bay and be as happy as anything. Next year you can swim, is the way you figure it. Probably about this time next year you'll be ready. Right now, you're just a little kid, but next year will be different.

The problem is to make your mother and father appreciate that. They don't seem very patient. It looks like they've been watching your cousin, the snotty little one everybody thinks is so cute. Half a year younger than you and she's swimming already. All the grownups are saying to you: "Don't worry. You'll be swimming any day now" – as if they think it really matters to you and they're trying to make you feel better. But you don't care. She paddles around and doesn't look all that great, when you come right down to it. She gets out of the water and shivers and pants and everybody crowds around her and tells her what a great job she's doing. You can watch it all; you have a great vantage point from the inflatable turtle out in the bay.

Quietly, when the grownups weren't around, you've spoken to her about the great big slimy things under the surface. At first she cried, which was good, but you got blamed for it. Even when you said you didn't hit her or anything, you still got scolded. Apparently when you get older, you get heck for things you just *say*. They all told her not to pay any attention to you and now she doesn't any more. She just sops up all the compliments she's getting just for thrashing around in the water.

And it's true that you're tempted by that–all the fuss people make. Your mother says she'll help you. She says it's easy. You just take off the armbands and she'll hold you for a while. Then, when she knows you're ready, she lets go but stays there just in case. You don't like the sound of the words "just in case," never have. But she says it will be fine. In no time you'll be swimming and people will be complimenting you, and maybe you'll get an extra dessert or two for a couple of days. It's tempting. But you know, deep down, that once you get off the inflatable turtle, anything can happen, especially with regard to the great, big slimy things down at the bottom.

✳　✳　✳

The water is not the only place where scary things are. Lots of them hide in the woods. Parents don't know about them because they only know what they read in books. For example, they say there are no leopards in the woods. They say leopards are only in Africa and there has never been one around here. But you can hear them just about every night.

Ever since you started going to the outhouse by yourself, you've been hearing the leopards. Of course, there are also bears, skunks, porcupines – great big porcupines – and snakes. You haven't seen any of them, but your uncle has, and he likes to tell about it before people tell him to stop telling stories because he'll frighten the children. Once there was a bear this big, and another year there was one even bigger. When your uncle was a boy, hardly any bigger than you, there was one time he was coming out of the outhouse and he heard this noise. He'd never heard a noise like that before, and just when he came around the corner in the path –

They always stop him right there, but you know what he's talking about. Leopards. You tried to ask him about it once, but he just said not to worry; he just likes to tell stories. That made you sure your mother had got to him. She knew that if the story about leopards got out, that would be the end of the cottage. You'd have to stay in the city, which wouldn't be so bad because at least you'd get to see some cartoons on Saturday morning. Your mother would hate that because she is always saying how great it is that you can have fun without cartoons on all the time.

Actually, it does seem to be fun a lot of the time, except when it's dark, the leopards are howling, and you have to go down the path by yourself. And there's no alternative. Last year you could casually ask if anybody else happened to be going down the path. You'd keep them company if they were. But this year is the year you do it by yourself. The snotty cousin, the one who can swim, she never goes down the path by herself, so that makes you bigger, at least at night.

Last night a toad jumped onto the path. You were really scared until you realized it was a toad. Then you thought: what if toads grew as big as dogs or leopards? Toads would be pretty scary then.

Maybe the most awful thing about cottages is you have to keep going places in the dark.

※　※　※

This summer was a big one:

You caught your third fish in history. Then your fourth and your fifth.

You ate two hamburgers and a hot dog once. Then had three pieces of cake.

One of your cousins taught you to make some funny noises that you can't make in front of your parents.

Your father saw an eagle and told you and you saw it too. It looked like just another bird, but your father said you would always remember it, and maybe you always will.

You didn't get poison ivy.

You learned how to play badminton, sort of. At least you learned how to serve and got a couple in, too.

One night you stayed up until ten-thirty and heard the grownups arguing about the prime minister.

Your mother let you walk around the golf course with her but she wouldn't let you play and you got tired of it, so you stopped after nine holes and your aunt took you home.

You learned how to row, and next year they say you will be able to do it with both oars at the same time.

❊   ❊   ❊

Every year you have to do something different at the cottage. They never let you stay the same, although they seem to stay the same themselves. Next year you are going to have to swim, no question about it. And your mother and father are going to kick you out of their room.

They don't put it that way. They say: "Next year, just think, you'll be able to sleep in the tent with the other kids!" When they say it they have that sound in their voices like you're supposed to be really happy. But what it means is you can't put your sleeping bag on the floor of your parents' room and they won't be right there in case something happens to come out of the woods and into the house. Now you're going to be off in the woods in a tent, and if there is a storm the tent will leak and a tree could fall on it if there is a big wind.

Even in the daytime the trees are scary. If you lie on your back and look up, all you can see is trees. In some places you can't even see the sky for all the trees. And they look, the way they waver, the way they sway back and forth, like they might fall right on top of you. In the nighttime, who's to stop them?

The worst thing about sleeping in the tent is that if you're scared you won't be able to say so because the other kids will laugh at you and call you a jamtart. Once you're big enough to sleep in the tent, you're too big to be scared. That's the rule. They always talk about the cousin who tried to go home in the middle of the night because he was scared and wound up off the path and sat down in the bushes crying until someone came and rescued him.

Still, the kids say they have lots of fun in the tent. They make noises and read comics and eat cookies that they have stashed away. Sometimes the mice come to eat the cookies and it is neat to watch them. Usually the kids can stay up later because the adults stop thinking about them once they are in bed and then they can't hear anything from the tent once they start arguing about the prime minister.

So it might not be too bad next summer. Some summer, it would be great just to stay the same and do the same things as last summer, but your parents want you to keep learning new things and you're going to have to put up with it for a few more years – at least until you've mastered swimming without the inflatable turtle.

The Teen Years

A Sudden Lack of Interest in Toads

One day a toad moved beside the path. As luck would have it, a father and his daughter were walking by. The father stopped.

"Look," he said. "A toad."

The daughter stopped and stared silently at the toad, which just sat there, as toads do. Finally, the daughter spoke.

"Dad?" she said.

The father quickly ran through his small supply of toad lore. Toads were a kind of frog. Or frogs were a kind of toad. Anyway. Toads were different from frogs because – because, because, because. Because toads didn't swim and frogs did. On the other hand, maybe toads *could* swim if they felt like it. A daughter would ask about that.

"What is it, sweetie?" he asked. Toads were different from frogs because, because, because: because they had either shorter legs or longer legs and drier skin. That might be it.

"What time is it?"

She was twelve. That was why. An invisible clock had begun to tick. She would not be interested in toads for a long time. It would be many years before she looked at a toad again. Her interest in toads would resume only when she had a daughter of her own. "Look, sweetie," she would say. "A toad!"

She had lost interest in toads because she had become a teen-ager. She had become a teen-ager at twelve, which is when most children become teen-agers, although some become teen-agers as early as nine. The record for the earliest instance of becoming a teen-ager is held by a little boy who asked Santa Claus for a brand name of sunglasses costing $150, at the age of four. The cottage is not for children who become teen-agers. Nothing at the cottage is of the slightest interest to them.

The reason the twelve-year-old girl wanted to know what time it was had to do with the possibility of a trip to the marina. Her uncle had said he might be going to the marina at three o'clock, to get propane and a newspaper, and she had asked if she could come along. Actually, she didn't ask. Because she was now, at the age of twelve, a teen-ager, she said "I'm going!" and looked defiantly around her, daring someone to contradict her. No one said anything, although her mother and father exchanged glances. A few minutes later they huddled in the pantry and wondered what was wrong.

"Don't worry," the father said. As a father, he knew he had a rapport with his daughter that a mother could never share. "I'll take her for a walk and find out what's on her mind." She had always loved going for walks in the woods with her father. He would point out things to her and she would ask adorable questions, such as: "How could you have dry skin if you were a toad?"

After lunch, he found her sprawled on the couch, inside the main house, with a Walkman on her head and reading a four-year-old fashion magazine. "It's a beautiful day outside," he said, trying not to sound judgemental. "How about a walk in the woods?"

"Now!?!" she replied.

At the onset of the age of twelve, teen-agers become unsuited for cottage life and become unsuitable at the cottage. The very things that attract their parents repel their children. These include:

1. The absence of modern appliances. Fathers love wood stoves because they don't have to cook on them. Mothers pretend

to love wood stoves because they love fathers. If mothers and fathers can't for some reason, such as better judgement, have a wood stove, then they pretend to love propane. Fathers also love the absence of dishwashers, vacuum cleaners, washers, and driers. "Isn't it quiet out here in the country?" the fathers exclaim. What that means for teen-agers is that they are going to have to do some work, for perhaps the first time in their lives. They will have to wash their own clothes, dry the dishes, sweep the floor.

In rare instances, television sets are also among the missing appliances. This creates another condition loved by parents and feared by teen-agers, namely . . .

2. Isolation from the modern world. Mothers and fathers stop watching the news They don't listen to the radio, they don't read the newspapers, except for the odd father who needs to know baseball scores or whether the dollar is worth anything. Parents know the modern world will still be waiting for them when they get back to it. Little of importance will have changed. In a day or two, at most, perhaps as little as one morning's coffee break, they will be caught up. They will know the news, the office gossip. In just a few minutes their anxieties and resentments will be back at pre-holiday levels.

Teen-agers of twelve don't know that. For them, anything could happen while they are away. They could come back to the city and find out that everyone but them is wearing green socks, for example. Because this does not happen in the adult world, adults forget what a disaster it is.

Another potential disaster area is the Top Forty, or the Fabulous Fifty, or whatever it's called in the city. In four weeks, three, or even two, the Top Forty could get out of control. The Beatles could reunite or the Loathsome Boils could break up. New stars could emerge that the cottage-bound children have never heard of. Established stars might sink out of sight. Or their friends might turn on them, for reasons that a person at the cottage cannot predict.

A twelve-year-old might leave the city content in the notion that her favourite group, The Whiny Boys, is immortal, at least for this year, only to return to the discovery that *nobody* likes The Whiny Boys any more and everybody has switched to The Sickly Sea Tortoises From Cleveland. It takes weeks to recapture the initiative after such a setback. Whiny Boys records have to be hidden at the back of the closet, Sickly Sea Tortoises From Cleveland records have to be purchased and their words memorized. Plus, there is a need to read up on the subject, find out which of the musicians used to be addicted to which substance, and why a band from Australia is named after a city in Ohio. In addition, there is the necessity of developing a reason why The Whiny Boys' latest record, now at the back of the closet, was not as good as their early stuff, recorded a year ago.

The importance of the marina to a twelve-year-old was in its status as link to the outside world. Other kids hung around there. They talked about still other kids who did interesting things with their lives, like owning boats that had 900-horsepower engines. They knew brand names of waterskis at the marina and talked about them at length. There was a guy who worked there, scooping the minnows out of a big tank for the Americans, and he knew a lot about what was going on. He was the first one to know that The Whiny Boys were not happening. Plus he had a haircut that was like short in one part and long in another and then short again.

Nothing much ever happened at the marina but the marina was where it was happening. They could all talk about how nothing much was happening and how they were looking forward to getting back to the city and whose junior high school was the toughest. And it was fun to do that. The marina was where a teen-ager could feel like a teen-ager instead of just someone who spent all her time with relatives.

Back at the cottage, there was the radio. But the radio stations in this part of the world were hopelessly out of date. Everybody at the marina said that. Like, the local station was just *discovering* The Whiny Boys. And anyway, you could never play it loud because everybody complained, even when it was only cranked up to 2.

The younger teen-agers looked up to the older teen-agers who complained even more about not having any fun. The older teen-agers were trying to have a social life and their parents said they weren't here to have a social life; they were here to enjoy being at the cottage. They were here to learn about the outdoors and to get to know their aunts and uncles better. The parents said they couldn't understand why the teen-agers said they didn't have fun at the cottage; the parents had fun at the cottage when *they* were teen-agers. But everybody knew parents were never really teen-agers.

Now they insisted that the teen-agers have fun the same way. Fishing was the worst. There was no way teen-agers could take the blaster along in the boat and play it, even at 1. Some uncle or a father would insist that the music scared the fish. Even talking scared the fish. And whistling scared the fish. But the motor didn't scare the fish. The motor was all smelly and noisy and the uncle smoked his pipe and that was smelly too. But that didn't scare the fish.

It was no teen-ager's idea of fun to go out in the boat without any music, away from other teen-agers, stuck with some uncle with a pipe you couldn't even talk to for fear of scaring the fish. Then even if the teens behaved themselves and didn't scare the fish, the fish didn't bite the hooks anyway. So what happened was a boring time. The uncle would say: "Look at that sunset!" or "Look at that loon!" But you know.

What the adults were really afraid of, and the teen-agers knew it too, was that some day the kids would go out by themselves with the blaster and catch all kinds of fish. Then every fishing boat would have a blaster in it and nobody would be able to complain. The adults weren't really afraid of scaring the fish. They were afraid of scaring the adults.

Fifteen years later the teen-agers would return with their children. They would tell the children what a good time they used to have fishing when they were children. And they would tell the children to turn their tape recorders down.

The Parental Years

Life with Dragons

At some point in their lives, cottage people awaken and discover they are parents. Usually it is when somebody calls out "Mommy" or "Daddy." From then on, the cottage looks different to them. They discover, for a few years, how low on the shelves the breakable things are, how easy it is to fall into the water, how far it is to the doctor. They discover how much more interesting the animals, the trees, the stars, and the toads are when they can be pointed out to a child. They also discover how much more complicated the animals, the trees, the stars, and the toads are when they have to answer questions about them. Such as:

"Is that the same star we saw yesterday?"

"How many stars are there?"

"Do toads like birds?"

"When did the water come?"

"Do bloodsuckers know when it's raining?"

With children around, the nature of the cottage changes for parents like the Frasers. Instead of getting away from it all, the Frasers are now taking quite a bit of it with them. They begin missing some of the creature comforts, the labour-saving devices they sneered at others for having at their cottages. On rainy days, they begin feeling sentimental about the city, and especially its washing machines.

The cottage and its environs take on a new and more sinister look when examined with a view to where tiny feet might land. The Frasers begin seeing risks where they used to see only a lake and a forest. They try not to speak too much of the risks in the lake and the forest, because the children are already seeing dragons there.

Somehow, despite everything, the forest and the lake become more appealing to the Frasers when they look at them through the children's eyes and see dragons. This is one of the mysteries of cottage life and it may have to do with the fact that dragons are not so bad, after what you see in the city. At the cottage, the worst things that can be found are dragons.

After hard days of helping the kids face the dragons, the Frasers wake up and realize how much the cottage means to them, how much they enjoy it. They start thinking about protecting it, wondering about how it will be used by their kids' kids. The light plays tricks on them. They turn a corner on the path and see their parents, their grandparents, people who have not been there for years. They see children who have not been there for years either, children who have become the Frasers.

Swatting mosquitoes, listening for childlike cries, alert for dragons, the Frasers know they enjoy what they become at the cottage and what their children become. All of the things that bothered them about the cottage as teens are the things they enjoy most now. One day they wake up after a quiet night and a quiet day and realize how much fun they are missing. Then they realize they are not missing it.

✳ ✳ ✳

Not all the parents on the lake are having as good a time, although many of them are going out more. For some of them, the lake represents a challenge they will never be able to meet. For others, the lake is an escape from their kids. For yet others, the lake is an extension of the city's social milieu. They are all out there, and they've brought the children.

Case No. 1: The worriers

The big day finally came for Buster when he was nine. "You're nine now, Buster," his father said, "and I think you're grown up enough."

So saying, his father took Buster's life preserver off. Buster had been swimming for three summers and now it was time. Now he could sit on the veranda without a life preserver. He could walk through the woods without a life preserver. He could go anywhere he wanted, within reason, without a life preserver.

No one asked what Buster thought about all this, but his parents were proud of him. When their friends asked them, as politely as they could, whether they were not being just a bit overprotective by requiring Buster to wear a life preserver all the time when he was at the cottage, Buster's parents were indignant. They pointed out that, ever since he had learned to swim, Buster had been allowed to go without a life jacket while inside the house.

Buster's parents believed that it was better to be safe than sorry. If a visitor raised an eyebrow when Buster wandered into the kitchen wearing his life preserver, Buster's parents would say that it was better to be safe than sorry. Then they would cite water disasters of which they had heard, ranging all the way back to the *Titanic*, which would not, they would argue, have lost so many passengers had more people made a habit of wearing life jackets all the time.

To be polite, visitors would often nod in agreement. To be polite, Buster's parents would then offer life jackets to the visitors, who, to be polite, would have to accept them. No one ever drowned at Buster's cottage. No one even came close. Of course, fewer and fewer people were coming to visit.

Buster's parents worried about Buster in the city. They had always worried about Buster, from the day he was born. Initially, when the idea of buying a cottage came up, Buster's parents worried that they shouldn't. Buster could fall or be bitten by something or get lost or fall into the water. He could get scratched by an overhanging branch. He could get poison ivy. In the end Buster's parents decided to buy the cottage, but that did not stop them from worrying, and they worried even more when Buster started to walk. The amount of harm that could befall Buster increased exponentially when he began walking. The only good thing about Buster learning to walk was that it meant he was big enough to wear a life preserver.

Buster's mother was brought up in the city. She was not afraid of the subway. Nor was she afraid of mice, German shepherds, or real estate agents. But she was afraid of gulls. The first time she went to a lake, she saw some gulls, which were not bothering anybody, and decided she was afraid of them. Over one long weekend, the woman who was to become Buster's mother learned to be afraid of many animals she did not see, as well as some she did—including the great blue heron, the pileated woodpecker, and any group of ducks larger than four. Buster's father was brought up in the suburbs. He was afraid of cows.

Case No. 2: The self-actualizers

George and Jim's parents arrive every year determined to have a vacation from George and Jim. All fall, winter, and spring in the city, they spend their time worrying about George and Jim. Now they are going to relax, get a suntan, do some swimming, have a beer, sail a bit, read, and make love more than they get a chance to in the city, what with one thing and another.

George and Jim's parents realize that it is difficult to have a vacation from George and Jim when George and Jim are there. But they try.

"You've got the whole lake to play with," they say. "How can you say there's nothing to do?"

When George points out that he is only three years old, and when seven-year-old Jim notes that Buster's parents never let him go to the dock without a life preserver on, the parents try a different approach.

"You can have such fun in the woods," they say. "There are so many fun things to do here, why don't you just explore?"

All around the lake there are lost children, out exploring. All around the lake are parents, unable to turn the page or make love, or turn the page *and* make love, because they are racked with guilt over children who may be lost in the woods.

Case No. 3: The improvers

Cynthia, Felicia, and Justin will never get lost in the woods. They are too busy at lessons. Among the three of them, they are taking sailing lessons, swimming lessons, water-skiing lessons, nature appreciation lessons, tennis, windsurfing and canoeing lessons, astronomy lessons, and aerobics exercises. The parents of Cynthia, Felicia, and Justin know there is no time to waste in their children's development, the summer least of all. So they enrol Cynthia, Felicia, and Justin in lessons over at the yacht club. There is no reason, the parents figure, why summer should not be a learning experience.

Cynthia, Felicia, and Justin have been told many times by their parents the reasons for all the lessons. "It's a jungle out there," they say. "You might as well prepare for it now." Cynthia, Felicia, and Justin know it's a jungle out there and that is why there is never time for them to walk in the woods. It is also why they never find George and Jim.

Case No. 4: The reincarnated

It is Jason and Jennifer's parents, Jason and Jennifer, who have a better chance of finding George and Jim, as they stumble around in the underbrush. Jason and Jennifer, along with their children, Jason and Jennifer, are out for a nature hike. Jason and Jennifer, the parents, represent a different type. It is their determined wish that Jason and Jennifer, the children, have exactly the same cottage experience that they had when they were growing up. Jason and Jennifer, the children, have their own ideas, but these do not, for the moment, count.

What the children would like to do is build a fort out of some old lumber left lying around from the new dock. They could put some branches on top of it and hide inside and no one would know they were there. But their father never built a fort when he was growing up at the cottage. He rubbed dirt on his face to make himself harder to see and played hide-and-seek with his cousins. Jason and Jennifer's mother never built a fort either. She went for nature hikes and learned about moss growing on only one side of the tree.

The difficulty Jason and Jennifer's parents have with wanting their children to have exactly the same experience is that their own experiences were different. That makes it difficult for Jason and Jennifer, hearing their parents argue about whether their children should play hide-and-seek or go looking for trees with moss on one side. One way or another, they usually wind up in the woods and find George and Jim.

※　　※　　※

Two or three times a summer, the parents get together. Jason and Jennifer's parents have a little bash on the 24th of May. They serve hors d'oeuvres and white wine and shoot off some fireworks. There is the bash at the yacht club on the July 1st weekend and the mid-August wine-and-cheese given by the parents of Cynthia, Felicia, and Justin to raise money for the recreational association.

Talk turns inevitably to the kids and how they compare with the kids of thirty years ago. This year there is chatter about Buster and how he is adjusting to life without a life jacket. The latest story about George and Jim getting lost is told. Jennifer and Jason's parents argue in front of everybody about whether Jennifer and Jason should relive their father's or their mother's childhood at the cottage. Buster's father inquires, as he always does, whether anyone has seen, lately, any cows in the woods. Cynthia's father is excited about the possibility of hiring a ballet instructor for next summer. They all agree the cottage is for the kids and wish only that it was easier to get a baby sitter.

That must be what happened to the Frasers. That must be why they are not here. Although they are a bit different. "They do a lot of staring out at the lake, looking at the sunset, that sort of thing," says Cynthia's father.

"She told me," says Cynthia's mother, "that after they've put the kids to bed, sometimes they don't even *talk*. They just sit there."

The Later Years

The Pressure on Grandpa

No one has ever grown old at the cottage. True, there are people there with white hair, but what does hair know? They are not old. If they are slower to get from here to there, it is because circumstances change at the cottage. Life there is not always the same for older people as it once was.

It is not because they are growing old; it is because their surroundings are different, somehow. Over time, paths grow steeper. The ground becomes less even. Extra roots appear, along the ground, and it is easy to trip over them. The landscape evolves, and the net effect is to make the land around the cottage more difficult to walk upon.

"Something will have to be done about these paths," the white-haired people say, upon returning from a stroll. The stroll has taken some time. It has taken more time than some of the younger people thought it would. They were, if the truth be known, just about to send out a search party.

The younger people want to say: "Where have you been? We've been worried about you?" But they know what the answer will be. It will be:

"Why? What's there to be worried about?"

And in fact there is nothing, other than the sheer fact of

oldness, to worry about. And nobody is old at the cottage. So the younger people say nothing.

Returning from the stroll, the strollers are not aware they have taken a long time. They know the paths are more difficult than they were. They also know that they enjoy them more. If it takes a bit longer to get around the path, it is because there is more to see on it and you wouldn't want to rush. The older people get, the more their eyesight declines, the more they see. The more they need a hearing aid, the more they hear on the path. The more their sense of smell deteriorates, the more they can smell in the woods. It is an amazing fact, but it happens, and it happens only at the cottage, not in the city. In the woods, the strollers see things others don't see, because they know where to look. They can hear the way the wind sounds blowing through the top of a white pine and they know when it sounds like rain.

Every once in a while, a stroller tells the others about his new powers. The others nod and, to themselves, smile. When the others are older, they will know. They will see and hear it for themselves. They will not hear "pass the salt, please," but they will hear the wind change direction. They will not recognize the five of diamonds without their glasses, but they will see the way a rabbit has nibbled on a young pine.

Not that everything will be wonderful for them. Many of the changes on the lake will be for the worse. The boats will go too fast and make too much noise. The storekeepers in town will be uncaring strangers, unlike their parents, who never asked for five pieces of identification, let alone one, before cashing a cheque. There will be fewer trees.

Out for a stroll, a stroller can look up to the sky and see the sky. And he can remember when he couldn't, when the size of the trees and the density of the forest was so great that all was dark underneath. That was when he and his cousins built a fort. Returning, late, from his stroll, the stroller will ask about forts, and why nobody ever builds them any more. Things were better, he will be thinking, when kids built forts. But he will not know exactly why things were better, so he won't say anything. A couple of weeks ago, when he said the same thing about coal oil lamps, people scoffed at him. So he will keep silent for the moment.

He knows that the children will listen to him. They will believe him about the trees and about the boats that towed the log booms up the lake. They will believe that there were more fish and that they were bigger. They will enjoy his stories about the Indians, and they will like it when he tells them about the animals on the island–how they are more afraid of people than people are of them; how the people and the animals can get along; how they always did.

※　※　※

Given the respect in which they are held, given their awesome potential power for good (or evil), few white-haired people spend as much time as they should studying up on the kinds of questions they will be asked. Nothing can be as disruptive to cottage life as an unprepared grandfather.

Bill's grandfather used to get everything wrong. He thought a poplar tree was a birch and a birch was something else. Sometimes a birch was a poplar; sometimes it was a weeping willow. Bill's grandfather had the only weeping willow in the history of the lake on his island, to hear him tell it. His grandchildren told it and people laughed at them.

He took the kids for walks in the woods and pointed out where the big snakes hung out and where the antelope played. He told the children completely unreliable stories about moss and claimed to be an expert on edible mushrooms and toadstools. Each day after one of those walks, the mothers sought out their children and, as subtly as possible, found out what their grandfather had told them. After this debriefing, the mothers took the mushrooms and toadstools on the pretense of trying to find the proper sauce to cook them in. Then they lost the mushrooms, by throwing them into the woods, and sadly reported that someone had thrown them out by mistake.

The children reported some of the other things Bill's grand-father had said, about the birch trees and the mosses, and their parents tried to provide alternative information, without actually contradicting him. But much of the information stuck, and was passed on down through the generations. That is why Bill still believes balsam trees attract ravens, for example, and it is why he is teaching his children always to put a saw down with the blade lying north-south.

Bill's grandfather was not the only one to have mistaken ideas. Until they get there, few people realize how difficult it is to be a grandfather at the cottage, how much pressure exists. It is not easy to come up with woods lore at the drop of a hat, particularly when most of one's life is spent in the suburbs, where there is no lore whatsoever, and no one would want it if there was any.

It is only natural, therefore, that some grandfathers begin making it up. Looking around the lake we can see many exam-ples of behaviour we cannot explain, and of which we may perhaps disapprove. It will make us more tolerant to know that much of it derives from some bit of lore passed down from a grandfather.

✻　✻　✻

Boats are more difficult to get in and out of than they used to be. The hills are much steeper, and the ground is not as solid as it was. There are not the great winds and storms that there were years ago, but there seems to be more of a chill at night. The water feels a bit colder, although heaven knows it was awfully cold fifty years ago. Still the children spent more time in it then than they do now. It's funny how that works. The children today will be saying the same thing fifty years from now, prob-ably – although it won't be the same thing as when we said it, or when our grandparents did.

Part 4

Cottage Man at Play

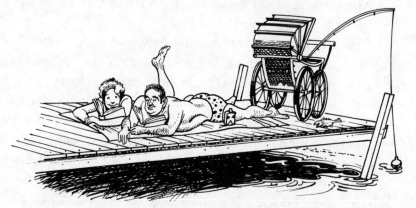

Fishing 1

Not Being Fashionable

As far as anyone can figure out, fishing has never been a trend, or even a fad. There has never been a magazine cover story called "The New Boom in Fishing." No person in the mental health industry has ever been called upon to view fishing with alarm. There has never been a magazine cover story called "The Growing Menace of Fishing." Newspapers have not done in-depth investigations. Psychologists have not been asked to explain what draws people to fishing. Social workers have not appeared on the noontime TV news alerting parents to the tell-tale symptoms to look for if they suspect their children might be fishing. The phenomenon has gone relatively un-examined, to the extent that it is possible it may not be a phenomenon at all.

It is interesting that this has happened, or not happened. As a food, fish is a phenomenon, a star of the Low-Cholesterol Decade. Fish, the food, is a cover story. You would think that people obsessed with recipes for fish might show some interest in the process by which fish become recipes. After all, salad eaters are often interested in gardening. On the other hand, people eat beef without, in most cases, showing any signs of wanting to become cattle ranchers or slaughterhouse employees.

And brunch fanatics rarely demonstrate any ambition to work in a hen house or a cheese factory, punching holes in the Swiss.

If fish is a phenomenon and fishing isn't, we must conclude that fish are more in vogue than fishermen. This is a strange thing to conclude, since the kind of fish that are in vogue are dead and the kind of fishermen who aren't, aren't. But if you examine the matter more closely, it makes sense. Start with the most important point. Fishermen do not wear outfits. You cannot be in vogue without an outfit.

Further, the recreational fishing scene is distinguished by no dance crazes or marketable songs. There are no identifiable fishermen heroes to endorse a line of cosmetics. There is no industry that can grow up around fishing, in the way that an industry could grow up around, say, aerobic exercise.

(One branch of fishing, fly fishing, is a slight exception to the rule, but it is hardly worth mentioning. Fly fishermen wear hip waders–meaning boots that come up to their hips, not boots that are hip. Fly fishermen – meaning fishermen who fish with flies, not fishermen who fish for flies; and by fishermen who fish with flies, we mean fishermen who use flies for bait, not fishermen who take flies along with them as fishing companions – fly fishermen wear hats with fly-casting lures stuck into them. So there is such a thing as a fly-fishing outfit. But it is not common around cottages, which are usually located on lakes, where fly fishing is rarely done. And even if it were, it is unlikely that a line of clothing based on rubber boots that come up to the hips could ever catch on, except with people too fashionable to think about such concepts as extreme discomfort.)

There used to be fishing outfits, but they were nothing much. You saw them in old magazine ads for Canadian cigarettes. Fishermen in old cigarette ads used to wear plaid shirts and thin moustaches. Now cigarettes and thin moustaches are out, and the plaid shirts have been replaced by whatever old thing you don't mind getting blood and fish guts all over.

Blood and fish guts hold the key to clever outfits never having been designed for fishing. Blood and fish guts are why fishing boutiques have not spread across the land. If disco dancers had been likely to get blood and fish guts all over them, they would not have bought those expensive disco outfits and disco would never have got off the ground.

In addition to blood and fish guts, fishermen are likely to have their clothes stained by motor oil, insect repellent, and parts of worm; they are likely to have to pull hooks out of their shirts. Because of this, fishermen have made the decision not to spend much money on their clothes, and a fishing togs industry has not arisen. For all the damage this may have caused to the economy, it has given some consolation to a few souls who like the idea of their being one place – a fishing boat – where they can be without worrying about being on the cutting edge of fashion.

The fishing industry, such as it is, gets by, content with its role of selling people warm socks, sinkers, rods, reels, artificial lures, and worms.

Fishing 2

Not Getting Started

Women who grow up with a cottage have an easy time making a decision about fishing. They can either decide they like it or decide they don't. Then, when later in life they meet a man who fishes, they can either fish with him or say: "I don't like fishing." Cottage Man, always a reasonable soul, will accept a statement like that about fishing if he knows it comes from someone who has actually tried it.

Establishing a position on fishing is more difficult for women who are not raised at a cottage, and marry into one. For each of these women, a decisive moment will arrive. She will be sitting in a boat with a fishing rod in her hand, minding her own business. Suddenly there will be a flurry of activity, shouts, splashes, and, out of the blue, as it were, a slimy thing with teeth will be flopping around her feet.

This moment is the reason people fish.

The woman having caught her first fish has two choices. She can pull up her feet and say "eek!" or she can pick up the nearest blunt object and hit the fish over the head with it, hold the fish up in the air, and say: "How's that?"

It is not an easy choice to make. Fortunately for them, men do not have to make it. Almost from birth, they know they have no choice. Men cannot say "eek!" It may be a biological thing; it may not. Either way, there is no percentage in it. While it may benefit some women in some situations to appear weak and feminine, these are not characteristics much demanded of men. At least not at the cottage.

Still, and not without reason, there are men who hate fishing. There is much to hate about it: the mosquitoes, the wind, the gasoline fumes, the slow pace, the fish. But such men are, until they find the right mate, condemned to live a lie, never admitting they don't like fishing, while at the same time never actually fishing.

"Not tonight," such men say, when approached for a post-supper troll; or, "I don't think I feel up to it right now." There are men who have said "Not tonight" every night for forty years, simply because they would not feel right saying they choose not to fish.

Even non-fishing men who are fortunate enough to mate with non-fishing women are not, so to speak, out of the woods. They may have children. If any of those children are male, they must be given the opportunity to learn fishing, probably with their fathers. If any of those children are female, they too must be given the opportunity to learn fishing, because modern thinking demands that the young women of today cannot be denied the opportunity to do the things their mothers and grand-mothers hated doing.

Modern thinking, when you come right down to it, has complicated matters for just about everybody. For example, there is a branch of modern thinking that not only condones non-fishing but identifies non-fishing boys as superior individuals. But even those who hope that their sons will turn out to be non-fishing boys cannot allow themselves to be deprived of the opportunity to be disappointed by them.

Some children, the sons and daughters of Brigitte Bardot-style animal-rights extremists, are taught that fishing is cruel and inhumane and that no one should ever wear a coat made out of the skin of a fish. Such children, when they rebel – as inevitably they must – turn to big game hunting, jacklighting deer, and March Break excursions to participate in the seal hunt. So parents must be careful what they attempt to teach their children about fishing. A wise course is a middle ground, such as telling the children that fish were put on this earth to provide low-cholesterol meals for man, and, as for being killed, they are kind of asking for it by biting at hooks with worms on them.

Fishing 3

Not Catching Anything

People fish for two reasons: to catch fish and to not catch fish. (A tiny fringe group has a third reason – to fish as a means of forgetting such worldly problems as split infinitives.) The frustration of the sport is that people rarely catch fish when they want to, and when they catch fish when they don't care if they do, they don't enjoy it all that much.

What sustains a child through the early fishing years is the constant sense of something being about to happen. Any second now a giant fish, a muskie, a huge pickerel, a big lake trout, is going to hit the line so hard you'll be lucky he doesn't pull you right into the water. That thought keeps you, the child, quiet in the boat. All you need is a stern glance from an adult to stop you in the middle of telling that joke your friend told you that you laughed at although you weren't quite sure what it meant.

Even if a giant fish doesn't strike, you could catch bottom, or weeds, weeds being preferable. Trolling along, perhaps letting your mind wander a bit, you could allow your hook to snag on a rock or a submerged log, and there would be a huge, long, slow, powerful tug. "I've got one! I've got one!" you would cry out and begin reeling in, only you couldn't, and a grownup would shout at you to let some line out and you wouldn't do it in time and your line would go suddenly slack and when you reeled it up your father's best red-and-white deep-diving River Runt would be gone.

"It was bottom," somebody would say, with what sounded like contempt.

"It wasn't! It was a big one!" you would reply, but in your heart you knew it was bottom. Bottom could be scary, so you would be quiet in the boat. Something could happen any minute. Something good or something scary.

Something good would be when the fish would bite, for real this time, you would somehow get it to the side of the boat, your father or mother would net it, kill it, show it to you, tell you what a good fish it was. Then you would head back to the cottage, arriving after dark, where everybody sitting around the fire would tell you what a big fish it was, even if it looked smaller in the living room than it did in the boat. Everybody would ask you whether it fought hard, if it jumped, if it dived under the boat. Somebody would take your picture holding the fish and you would maybe hold it out just a bit from your body to make it look a little bigger in the picture. You would put up with an hour's worth of silence in the boat for that.

Sometimes nothing would happen, day after day, night after night. It was possible to give up fishing then. Or it was possible to begin enjoying nothing happening, a feeling that signalled the impending arrival of adulthood.

The sense of nothing about to happen sustains people who just like to go for a ride on the lake but want the ride to be slow. In addition, they may feel that they should be *doing something* at the same time. In modern thinking, there is no time to waste, even on holidays. Those suffused with modern thinking carry things with them in the boat – if not fishing rods, then cameras.

With a fishing rod in hand in a quiet boat, a man or a woman, or a man *and* a woman, can glide quietly through the sunset watching out for turtles, beavers, herons, porcupines, lily pads, clouds, moss, and ferns–all this without the slightest worry about wasting time.

For that constant sense of nothing being about to happen there is only one proper boat – a canoe. It is true that within a limited amount of time – say, between the end of the evening meal and the onset of darkness – a canoe will not get you very far. But then, the object is not to get anywhere, just as the object is not to catch fish, just as the object is to have no object at all. If there is no object at all, it is better to be without the sound of an engine and the smell of gasoline.

Returning about dark, just as the mosquitoes are biting and the fish are not, it is possible to provide a plausible and sincere explanation of where you were and what you were doing.

"We were fishing," is what you say, and you may even believe it. You can moan a bit about the fact that they aren't biting this year. You can invite debate on the age-old topic of live bait versus artificial lures. You can even, if you feel you must, mutter about acid rain and whatnot. The fact is, you didn't catch any fish and you had a wonderful time.

You must remember to give no inkling of that. It is an ironclad rule of cottage life that couples, if they are to go out together in boats, must fish, take pictures, or count species of birds. If they come back and say they were just out enjoying the sunset, people will assume they were having a serious conversation and are splitting up.

Fishing 4

Reasons for Not Catching Anything

The fishing was always better last year and it was always better the week before you arrived. The fishing has an uncanny way of knowing your schedule. People do not explain it that way, however. They say the water is too warm, or it is too cold. Usually it is too warm. When the water is too warm, the fish stay at the bottom where the water is cooler. If you fish near the bottom and don't catch anything, it is because the fish are so lazy in the warm weather that they cannot be bothered to bite anything.

It is useful to remember that there are many more reasons for the fish *not* biting. If the fish are biting, there is only one explanation: the skill of the fisherman.

There are other reasons why the fish aren't biting. The lake is fished out, often by the tourists. Tourists are people who are around for a matter of days, as opposed to you, who are around for a matter of weeks. As mentioned, acid rain may be to blame, as well as the effluents being discharged by industrial operations hundreds of miles away.

Live bait is not working this time of year. They were biting like crazy on worms last week, but not any more. The low water level has caused the fish to change their habits. There may be a plague of something – eels, perhaps, or Americans. And there is always the lunar influence, which is hard to measure, exactly, but should not be discounted.

Fortunately, while there are many reasons why the fishing is off, it will recover. It always does, until just before you arrive.

Ski vs. Sail

A Rapid Onset of Speed

A waterskier stands behind a boat going at high speed. One person drives the boat. Another looks back at the waterskier. For this audience of one, the waterskier tries to do tricks, while he holds on for dear life.

A windsurfer stands on a board and holds onto a sail. The wind drives him. He is too far away from land for anyone to see him do tricks. Anyway, the trick is to hold on for dear life.

Cottage World is divided between waterskiers and windsurfers. Waterskiers like noise and speed. Windsurfers like the sound the wind makes and don't want to go any faster than the wind will allow them.

Waterskiing advocates say they can go 45 miles per hour on one ski. Windsurfing advocates say they don't pollute, and they don't make noise, and neither do their boards.

There are arguments to be made on both sides. Waterskiing is fun to watch, particularly if no one you care about is doing it. The little children enjoy bobbing in the waves made by the boat as it nearly runs into the dock. When they grow up a little, there is a great feeling of accomplishment in being able to "get up," as being successfully pulled out of the water on skis is called. Getting up is a rite of passage, a builder of self-confidence.

Unfortunately, it is also the highlight of the waterskiing career. Everything to follow is, if not literally downhill, at least less exciting. The child, once he successfully gets up, finds out that it is easy, and a bit tiring, just to stand there behind the boat. He learns that he must do tricks in order to amuse himself and those in the boat who are his travelling audience and the only witnesses to his skill, or lack thereof.

So the new skier goes outside the wake, drops one ski, passes the rope around his back and under his knees. He learns to smile at the people in the boat while he is doing these tricks. A few times he falls, which seems to bring about a more sympathetic response from his cottage mates, because falling in the water behind a fast boat is like falling on the sidewalk, only wetter and with less chance of encountering pigeon droppings.

Although all sensible people come to realize the essential emptiness of waterskiing, many of them, particularly men, and particularly later in life, feel compelled to try it again. It becomes a rite of passage again, although this time it might be termed a rite of non-passage. The would-be skiers want to prove that they are *not* older. Often, in attempting to get up, they get only wet, and attempt to blame this fact on the boat.

It is not that failed skiers are fatter. Rather, as they point out, it is a case of today's boats not being as powerful as the boats of the failed skier's youth. Reminded that today's boats have three times the horsepower of the one that got him up twenty years ago, the failed skier ventures the opinion that horsepower today is not the same.

Secretly, the would-be skier is glad that he failed. He notices that the new motors, although much weaker, seem to make the skiers go very fast, and that when the skiers go very fast they fall very hard. Having failed, however, the failed skier does not turn automatically to windsurfing.

❋   ❋   ❋

Windsurfing, while not dangerous, is hard work. The sail falls into the water, and with the sail goes the person who is holding

on to it at the time. Once back on the board, the sailor has to
lift up the sail, which contains large and heavy amounts of water,
which have to be lifted with it. Once the lift has been successfully
completed, the position of the sail causes the weight of the board
to shift. This can cause the person standing on it to fall, dropping
the sail into the water, from which it must be lifted again, once
the person who has dropped it has lifted himself out of the
water. It is a far less thrilling process than waterskiing and takes
a different personality type.

The process by which the sail is alternately lifted and
dropped is difficult at the best of times. The best of times are
times at which there is no wind. At such times, the sailor must
contend only with the weight of the sail, the weight of the
water, and his own sense of balance. Unfortunately, windsurfing
is not done at the the best of times, since windsurfing requires
wind. Without wind, the windsurfer stands still on a board in
the lake, not surfing, not even moving, feeling stupid, with
people yelling sarcastic things like: "That's really good!"

With no wind, there is a degree of stability involved that
is attractive to someone of a certain personality type. However,
people of that personality type are probably up in the cottage
having a nap. Windsurfers want wind.

But when they get it, a further element of instability is
added to a vehicle that does not need it. The sail must be lifted
(along with the water on it), the sailor must keep his balance
from shifting so much that he falls into the water, drops the sail,
and has to start all over again. Now, when the sail is successfully
lifted, the wind begins to blow on it, causing the board to move,
sometimes in the intended direction, sometimes not. Either way
it is moving, and standing on it is not easy.

The literature of windsurfing speaks of serenity, of quiet
voyages across the wind. The cinema of windsurfing, which so
far consists mainly of beer commercials, shows boards moving
swiftly, but silently, in front of the sunset, accompanied by nice
music. The neophyte windsurfer believes it all, until he falls,

again and again, rises again and again, lifts the sail again and again, and again and again, falls. He then becomes angry.

Naturally his anger is directed at the board and the sail. His colourful shouts at them shatter the silence and pierce the serenity. He is angry at the wind too, which he calls a stupid so-and-so. His back hurts.

The literature of windsurfing reminds him about it not polluting. His intellect tells him he is better off doing this than waterskiing. But he is cold and his shoulders hurt. Soon someone will come and get him in the boat and tow him back to shore, where he can be dry and warm and humiliated. At least with waterskiing, he could fake an injury. But windsurfer injuries are of no value, it being the conventional wisdom that they are caused by clumsiness and incompetence.

The inferiority feelings of the novice windsurfer increase each year as the skills of the experts improve. Whereas windsurfers once thought it was not only nice but a major accomplishment to sail quietly across the lake in the breeze, now they want to make the board jump up in the air. They want to do handstands on the board, spin around on it, hold on one-handed, and wave to their friends. They enter competitions and race. They do fancy stunts and are judged and scored. Where once there was only a person, a board, and the wind, now there is competition.

The remainder of the progression is familiar. Soon, boards will sport hostile-looking pictures and names. Like cars, they will become cougars and panthers and challengers and darts and destroyers. Inevitably, it will happen and you will know the end is near when you see it: somebody puts a motor on a windsurfer.

You will know the end has arrived when someone skis behind it.

Books

Great Thoughts with Sunglasses On

Many cottages are not blessed with television. At those cottages, those who want to do something without moving much but without necessarily sleeping either, are forced to read. Reading, which is something not done much in the city, consists of sitting down, holding a book, and turning a new page every minute or so. It can also be done lying down. Since people's reading skills become rusty over the winter, intense preparation for the summer reading season is necessary.

Part of the preparation, particularly for the reader who is getting on a bit, involves the choice of proper eyewear. The most fruitful summer reading takes place on a dock. The reading is not fruitful because there are matters of consequence in the book; the reading is fruitful because a suntan can be acquired at the same time. In the city, acquiring a suntan is simple: a person sits on a bench at noon-hour, closes his eyes, tilts his head towards the sky, and holds a reflecting device under his chin. This is considered a constructive activity, because it does not take place on company time and because a suntan gives its owner a feeling of confidence and is therefore an asset in business meetings.

However, busy summer people cannot just sit there. Nor

can they just lie there, passively, and let the sun tan them. They need to accomplish something else at the same time, and reading is it.

In many cases, dock reading involves books about how to earn money. Such books are not time-wasting, because earning money is thought to be a fruitful activity and learning about earning money is thought to be almost as fruitful, particularly if it entails sun-tanning at the same time.

Because sun-tanning is an essential aspect of summer reading, the reader must maintain the proper attitude vis-à-vis the sun. Most summer readers prefer to deal with the sun head-on. The chair must be placed in such a way as to allow the reader to tan his face and the front of his body while reading. This allows the pages of the book to be in shade, and sunglasses need not necessarily be employed. If the reader, however, feels it necessary to look up at the scenery from time to time – for example, to see if a boatload of visitors is approaching or a storm is brewing in the west – he may need sunglasses. If he is to read with the sunglasses and he is getting on a bit, he will need prescription sunglasses, which make it difficult to see unblurred storms approaching from the west.

In the city, people who are getting on a bit use half-glasses. On the dock, half-sunglasses are impossible, because half-sunglasses have not been invented. Society, experts on this sort of thing say, has been too busy inventing other things, such as nuclear submarines and kiwi-fruit popsicles, to invent half-sunglasses. The extent to which society has fallen behind in this respect is demonstrated by the fact that society does not know whether to call them half-sunglasses or sun-half-glasses.

Whichever they are, it makes summer reading a chancy business, involving as it does the possibility of boatloads of people approaching unnoticed, disguised as blurs on or near the horizon.

Another potential difficulty with summer reading involves the likelihood of unusual suntans. The same kind of person who could benefit from half-sunglasses or sun-half-glasses often finds that wrinkles appear on his stomach when he sits down on the dock to read. This is not, in itself, humiliating, except that the wrinkles, when a suntan is finally acquired, take the form of white lines, marking exactly those spots where the sun does not shine. To avoid this, a sun-tanner could lie on his back, but this would involve squinting into the sun; or he could lie on his front, but this would involve a sunburned back of the head.

Summer reading, hardened and darkened verterans know, is not as easy as it looks.

It has been established that preparation helps. Part of the preparation involves the buying of books. Veteran summer readers know that reading can not all be fun. They learned this in school. If reading is fun, there is something wrong about it. The book being read is probably not likely to enhance the person reading it. On the other hand, fruitful books–which are usually books about dead politicians or books about how to make money–are not always totally enjoyable. So the veteran summer reader learns to make compromises. He makes certain to buy at least one book he can talk about when he returns to the city–a book about a corporation or an environmental hazard, or a corporation that is an environmental hazard.

By reading such a book or at least reading enough of it to be able to talk about it, he deals with the guilt he might otherwise have felt for reading spy stories, mysteries, and lurid potboilers.

Books of that type are not the sort a person would want to be seen reading on the bus to the office. On the other hand, books of a serious nature are usually too expensive to be allowed onto the dock, where they will inevitably be covered with oil slicks from suntan lotion and red stains that were once insects. When you add them up, there are more reasons than you would have thought to avoid reading the kinds of books a person would want other people to think he is reading. It becomes necessary, then, to invent a rationale for reading the kinds of books a person would have wanted to read in the first place.

One thought is that there is much useful information in the books that are normally thought of as junk reading. Spenser, the Boston detective in the Spenser books, has a recipe for corn bread. Further, Spenser is likely to say profound things on the subject of food, such as his observation that "buffalo stew tastes very much like beef stew."

Unlike other summer detectives, such as Philip Marlowe and Sam Spade, Spenser has no discernible first name, which lack is probably of metaphorical significance and can be talked about in the city by a summer reader with sufficient gall. And to top it all off, Spenser's friend and helpmate, who is called Hawk, reveals that baby oil will take the saltwater corrosion off a .357, in case you happen to have a .357 lying around, whatever one is.

Helen MacInnes, a thriller writer, can also be read without guilt, in part because of her definition of disinformation: "It includes a fact or two to make a story credible, then adds the distortions." Such information can come in handy at the office. In Anthony Hyde's book *The Red Fox*, there is a discussion of provisional adoption statutes. In *The Handmaid's Tale*, by Margaret Atwood, we learn that the traditional distress call of Mayday comes from the French *m'aidez*. All of these are books we would have read anyway. What a bonus to learn that they actually contain information, since the acquisition of information is, to many people, what reading is all about.

John Irving, in *The Cider House Rules*, tells of the symptoms of the disease eclampsia, as well as the way to treat it ("bed rest, diet, reduction of fluid intake . . ."). John Le Carré, in *A Perfect Spy*, gives tips on how to sneak into a room we are not supposed to be sneaking into: "Tread heavily, she tells herself, remembering her training. If you have to make a noise, make a bold one." Le Carré also reveals that it is "standard intelligence practice to continue transmitting whether or not the party is listening at the other end."

On the political side, the British political junk novelist and bon vivant, Jeffrey Archer, lets slip the information that government members of Parliament who expect to be named to the cabinet wait by the phone for forty-eight hours after a general election. "If the phone hasn't rung by then," Archer writes, "they remain on the back benches."

While you are on the dock, ostensibly getting a suntan and not being up to much, you are learning about the British parliamentary system, the derivation of Mayday, and the proper method of oiling a .357. And all along, people thought you were wasting your time.

It is necessary to point out that there is good advice in great books as well. To thine own self be true, neither a borrower nor a lender be, never send to know for whom the bell tolls, and so on. Still, some thoughts are too profound to be encountered with sunglasses on.

Games

Pain in the Name of Fun

Early on in the history of cottaging someone decided that there should be games. People should not just sit there reading books. They should not just canoe around admiring rocks and trees. They should not just fish and lie in hammocks and stroll through the woods. They should play games and have fun.

Someone, very early on, decided that having fun and playing games was the same thing. This may have been a caveman. In cave days, games had just been invented and their novelty had not worn off. People still liked to play games. Considering the alternatives, this made some sense. Since there were no hammocks or books, the alternatives to games, for the cave people, consisted to being chased by flying reptiles and trying to invent fire. The alternatives for women were the same, except for being dragged around by the hair, next to which even volleyball seemed refined.

So we probably have the cavemen to blame for games. When they left the cave to go to the cottage, which consisted of another cave, but closer to the river, they took the concept of games with them. For the types of cottage games we play, however, we have only ourselves, and a few more recent ancestors, to blame.

When the modern ground rules for cottage games were being laid down, someone decided that people who, because of age, infirmity, or disposition, would not dream of playing games in the city would play games at the cottage. They would take their bad backs, their trick knees, their arthritis, and their rheumatism out to the badminton court, there to trip over roots, stumble and fall, pull muscles, twist knees, and put backs out, all in the name of being a good sport, all in the name of fun.

Neither children nor adults train for the cottage. They do not begin a strict regimen of drills preceded by lengthy loosening-up exercises. They do not buy the proper footgear. They do not observe the proper diet. They just arrive, somebody gets out the badminton gear, and away they go, charging back and forth, puffing audibly, and sprawling in the dust, or mud, depending upon weather conditions.

At the cottage nobody says: "Sorry, I'm too old for that." At the cottage nobody thinks he *is* too old for it. Nobody thinks he is too old for anything. As a consequence, within three days of their arrival many sportsmen and sportswomen are nursing bruises, scrapes, pulled hamstrings, sore knees, aching backs, and suspicious twinges here and there. To make matters worse, wiser people than they solicitously ask after their health and issue gentle and belated warnings about overdoing it.

The beauty of badminton

Badminton is the ideal cottage game. It requires little space and almost no equipment. Theoretically it involves no physical contact. In many games, the ball will hurt a player if it hits him. In badminton, the ball – which is called a bird, is not round, and has feathers – will not hurt. Distances to be run are not formidable. A badminton player can cover the entire court in a few quick strides. It is true that an older player, once having taken a few quick strides, often takes a few more than he should because of a difficulty in stopping. It is this that causes the tumbles into the bush that are fondly recalled every year, and it is this that causes the net to be knocked over at least once a game by a hard-charging veteran player.

Strategically, the game allows older players to keep up with younger players by being smarter about tactics. Later on, it allows the younger players to overcome the older players by being faster and stronger. It also allows the older players to convince themselves that the younger players only win because they are luckier.

Badminton comes with a range of built-in excuses for the loser. There is the sun, which is in the eyes of the losing player. Badminton is always played at sunset, for reasons that must be clear to the inventors of the game but are obscure now. When players change sides midway through a game, so as to neutralize the effects of the sun, the sun disappears behind a cloud to allow one player – usually the younger one – to be luckier than the other.

If it were not for the sun, the older player would win. The sun, however, is not the only factor in the losses suffered by deserving players. Wind is also important. Although it is thought, by the uninitiated, to have a predictable effect, always blowing in the face of one player or to the backhand of another, it in fact swirls unpredictably, often forcing the shots of one player to go long, then suddenly dying, just when the player has adjusted for the wind, causing his shots to fall into the net. Because of such environmental factors, badminton is an extremely difficult game to win. However, moral victories are quite easily obtained.

The glories of golf

Moral victories are also available at the golf course, but a bit of humiliation must be endured at first. Strictly speaking, golf courses are not part of the cottage proper, but there is always one nearby. There, the cottager suffers the scornful glares of the members, who are properly dressed. He suffers the heat, which is always worse than back at the cottage. He suffers the wind, which, unaccountably, is worse too. He suffers the rough, which resembles the woods. He suffers the score.

Back at the cottage, they think he's having a pleasant little outing, a lazy day on the golf course. When he gets back, he'll be eager to get to those chores he postponed, perhaps fix those broken boards on the roof or help paint the ceiling.

They don't know he's suffering out there on the golf course. They don't know he's only doing this because it's tradition, because his father did it, and his father's father before that. Every year there has to be a golf game, no matter how much it hurts.

Every year, the golf game is the same. The golfers, picking up the clubs for the first time since last summer, expect to match their best-ever score, which was accomplished at the age of seventeen. Decades of exposure to the course have built up a store of memories, with most of the bad ones filtered out. Arriving at a precise spot on a precise hole, the summer golfer can remember exactly what club he used to reach the green, shooting clear over that tree there, five years ago – or was it ten? Or was it twenty? Tricks of the mind have removed the memories of the ball, struck with precisely the same club, hitting the tree and bouncing back, almost at the golfer's feet, yet somehow incapable of being found.

Trudging through what is called the rough, but is really thick underbrush full of boulders, the summer golfer looks for his ball and for the club he tossed in its general direction. It occurs to him that the tree might, over the years, have grown. He curses the tree. Without really wanting to, he recognizes that the only part of his game that has survived from age seventeen is his temper. Insects are biting him, bushes are scratching him, and he is not enjoying his own company very much. Worse, he knows he will be living through the experience again next summer because he lacks the inner security that would allow him to give it up.

Back at the cottage, they don't suspect his mood. They

don't know his aches ache and his pains pain, that he has new aches and new pains and that they hurt. When he comes back and just wants to lie down for a while, they don't understand. They think he's (a) rested and (b) lazy.

The vanity of volleyball

Volleyball started at the cottage as a simple game, the object of which as to keep the ball in the air as long as possible. People would pat the ball around for a while, keep score if it occurred to them, then go for a swim. Then volleyball went to California.

When it came back, it was a different game. Volleyball had gone Hollywood. In order to play it properly, people had to be tall, blond, and wear flowered shorts that reached below the knee. Specialization developed. Short blond people would keep the ball from hitting the ground, hit it to other short blond people, who would hit it gently up in the air. Tall blond people would leap into the air and with their fists hit it down at the players on the other side of the net, then all the players on that side would run around slapping each others' hands.

When that version of volleyball came to the cottage, the short blond players quickly became jealous of the tall blond players, some of whom were not blond anyway, the cottage not being in California. The short players wanted to play up near the net and hit the ball straight down with their fists so they could slap hands with all the other people on their team. The people on the other side of the net, some of whom were little girls, realized, after a while, that they were going to get hit with the ball and that the ball was going to hurt them. They asked if they could play volleyball with a balloon instead, and, when the tall blond guys said no, the little girls said the hell with it.

At the cottage, no game can be played without the consent and co-operation of the little girls. Such is the manpower situation. Right now, the volleyball net is at the back of a closet somewhere and the little girls are playing soccer with the volleyball.

The temptation of targets

One year somebody brought a BB gun. Another year it was a powerful slingshot. A couple of years after that it was a bow and arrow. The idea is to shoot at a target. The reality is that the pellets, the stones, and the arrows hit trees, causing, in the minds of some of the tree fans around, irreparable damage and posing a threat to the ecology of the cottage.

Target shooters are always careful to avoid shooting at animals, but on rare occasions someone accidentally hits a squirrel or a crow, thinking that squirrels and crows don't count. Thus endeth the target shooting.

Night games

When more than one family uses a cottage, there is a rule that games must be played after dark. This has to do with the lack of television, and with what some people see as the absolute necessity of being sociable. This, along with inferior lighting, precludes the reading of books.

The games to be played vary from cottage to cottage, from province to province. Often the game is a variant of rummy. Sometimes it is hearts. But each cottage has a game. It is The Cottage Game, and it is played because it has always been played. Sometimes people like The Game, which helps. It is not essential, however. Peer pressure will ensure that there are always enough players.

"What do you mean, you're going to skip The Game? You *can't* skip The Game! *Nobody* skips The Game!"

So it is that a grown man finds himself, for the fifteenth night in a row, involved in the game of poker, in which the chips are black-eyed peas, in which threes are always wild, in which a flush beats a full house and two pairs beat three of a kind.

From time to time an outsider participates in The Game and points out that two pairs do not, in real poker, beat three of a kind. It is pointed out to him that two pairs have always beaten three of a kind *here*. And when he tries to deal a game in which twos are wild, people look at him as if he is crazy.

The morality of Monopoly

At such a time, he may be tempted to join the children, who are playing their fifth Monopoly game of the day. Parents rarely think about their children playing five Monopoly games a day when they look forward to the joys of the cottage. They think of a summer spent without television. They think of nature walks, fishing expeditions. They forget that it is the nature of children to beg off nature walks and fishing expeditions because they are in the middle of a Monopoly game.

The game has become cut throat over the years, developing a set of under-the-table rules that would have amazed the Bros. Parker. Wheeling and dealing goes on at all times, regardless of whose turn it is. Get-out-of-jail cards are sold at cut-rate prices. Trading arrangements are arrived at, aimed at blocking certain players from ever owning Ventnor Boulevard and the other yellow properties. Railroads are traded for future considerations.

The children have a new board, which they are enjoying, barely noticing the fact that it is in French. A well-meaning relative, thinking to sneak in something that will help them improve themselves over the summer, bought the game, and the children thanked him profusely. Since they know the game so well, they continue to play it in English, saying "St. James" instead of "St. Jacques" and recognizing, without having to read it, the Community Chest card that says they have won second prize in a beauty contest, collect $10.

The science of Scrabble

There is an uncle who always arrives with the latest games. Over the years, some of his gifts to the cottage involved various plastic devices that hurled plastic projectiles upwards or outwards. The projectiles eventually found their way into the forest and the flinging devices are at the bottom of the closet. Others of the latest games were board games. Most of them are now on a low shelf, underneath the other ones. The kids looked at them, tried to read the rules, and went back to Monopoly. Scrabble lasted, though.

It lasted with the adults, who turn to it when the rummy game gets too noisy. At a cottage, Scrabble is not an easy game to keep intact. There are cracks and holes, and letters keep falling into them. Every so often, someone notices that no one has made a word including the letter *J* all summer, and a new set is purchased. The discussions that highlight the game are not new:

"I thought italicized words were all right."

"It's *muddying* not *mudding*. I don't think *mudding* is a word. And if it is, it only has one *D*."

"Q-A-Y. I'm sure that's how they spell it."

"It's a Greek letter. We always use Greek letters."

"I'm thinking."

"Eighteen points! You're going to take the triple word for eighteen points?"

"Z-O-O-N. It's the singular of Z-O-A. Or the plural."

"Do you have to get a seven-letter word every time? You've been sitting there for twenty minutes."

"I'm thinking."

The beauty of Scrabble, aside from its inherent virtues, is that when non-players look over at the Scrabble table, they think something intellectual is going on.

The solace of solitaire

In the city, the joys of solitaire have been superseded by modern, cosmopolitan pursuits, such as learning to store recipes on a home computer or watching videotapes of old Mickey Rooney movies on the VCR. People think there are constructive things to do with their time and think that playing cards by themselves is a waste of it. Furthermore, solitaire has the image of being played only by losers and lonely people. Now lonely people go to singles bars and computer dating services. When they come home, alone, they are too tired to play solitaire.

It is a success-oriented society, and no award has ever been given to a solitaire player. There are no solitaire leagues, no solitaire champion. Solitaire is never written about, never seen on television – not even on all-sports networks, which show everything else, and not on public television stations, which show bridge.

The cottage, in all but a few instances, is not a success-oriented place, and people play solitaire there. They will deal the cards out, just as they always have, just as their parents and their grandparents have, and they will talk to the cards as they play them.

"Well, that's stupid," they will say, when a five turns up instead of the ace they wanted.

"Isn't that nice?" they will ask themselves when a deuce turns over just where they wanted it.

No one else in the room answers, because no one else hears, each being busy talking to his own cards.

Each solitaire player has his own game. Sometimes a visitor will bring a new one, and sometimes the new game will be adopted. Some games are harder to win than others. A player winning one of the hard ones will loudly announce his triumph to the others, who will fail to notice.

Calm prevails in a room full of solitaire players. Tempers rarely flare and voices are hardly ever raised. The worst possible occurrence is the discovery, on the part of one of the players, that he has been playing with a fifty-one-card deck. (It is an axiom of cottage solitaire that there is never more than one card missing.)

Fortunately, many solitaire games are constructed in such a way that a player never knows that he is playing with less than a full deck, and many people happily spend many a summer evening in that fashion.

The peace of puzzles

Every two years, when George and Jim's great-aunt Sybil visits from England, she demands that someone find her the jigsaw puzzle of Van Gogh's sunflowers. Three pieces are missing in the sunflower, but Aunt Sybil knows that and it doesn't bother her. It is stuck in her memory that she and her sisters did the sunflower puzzle every year when they were growing up, and she is determined to do it each year she is here.

The sunflower puzzle means the cottage to George and Jim's great-aunt Sybil.

It is a slightly different puzzle that Sybil puts together now. The one she did with her sisters had only 74 pieces and was made of wood. This one has 750 pieces – 747, actually – and it is made of not-very-sturdy cardboard. But it is still the sunflower: the most beautiful picture ever painted, according to Sybil, and the best puzzle every jigsawed.

Others at the cottage are less loyal than great-aunt Sybil. Most Christmases someone remembers the cottage and gives a puzzle for a gift. Many of these puzzles are, like many Christmas gifts, picked up in airport gift shops at the last minute. Consequently, many of the cottage jigsaw pictures are of such things as Lake Louise, Portage Avenue at night, and a member of the Royal Canadian Mounted Police on horseback in front of the Parliament Buildings. Each puzzle eventually enters cottage tradition, usually a few years after it enters the floor of the closet, minus three pieces.

Jigsaw puzzles are best done by the very young, whose eyes have not begun to deteriorate, and the very old, who have exactly the eyeglasses they need. Middle-aged cottagers can still see well up close or far away, but not both. What remains of their eyesight is protected by a kind of vanity that does not go well with the solving of jigsaw puzzles. Squinting around a card-table in inadequate light, they are uncertain as to whether to look through or over their half-glasses, and are no use at all.

Eventually, nostalgia clouds the memory the way moisture clouds the glasses and they all remember how good they were at solving the puzzles of years gone by. They will remember them vividly and lament the fact that no one makes puzzles like the one of Portage Avenue at night any more.

Canoes

The Thrill of Slowing Down

Canoeists on the lake always talk to each other as they pass. What they say is not particularly interesting. "Nice night. Yes, isn't it?" But they always talk because they recognize each other as members of a breed. They are among the few people remaining on earth who are not interested in going fast.

There was a time, during the bicycle revival of the seventies, when it was thought that bicyclists were like that too. And for a time they were, chugging aimlessly along the side streets and bicycle paths, slowing to watch the leaves turn, ready to stop at any moment to admire a sunset or a family of ducks in the water. But the moment passed. Bicyclists bought shiny pants and helmets with rearview mirrors. They bought bicycles with twenty-seven gears, to which they attached plastic bottles so that they would not have to stop to have a sip of water. They roared down the bicycle paths, looking neither to left nor right, frightening dogs and children and intimidating bus drivers.

When they got to the lake, they did not get into canoes. They might have tried once or twice. It is possible to make a canoe go pretty fast. But a canoe, all rounded bottom and gently curving sides, lacks the high-tech aggressive look of a bicycle. A person would look silly putting on shiny pants and a helmet to try to make a canoe go fast. Which is why people in canoes do not wear helmets, why they go slowly and stop to talk to each other.

Even when canoes do go fast, when they rock rapidly through white water, they are still canoes. They are not speedboats or twenty-seven-speed bicycles. It is not the canoe that provides the power; it is the water. The canoe rides the water and its occupants humbly steer.

The canoe is restful for short distances, tiring for long. It is hard work against the wind, difficult to balance across the wind, and somebody always wants to sing a song – one purportedly sung by the voyageurs – to help keep the stroke. Not enough summer people can sing and paddle at the same time.

The canoe has changed. It has gone from cedar strip to aluminum to fibreglass. There are large towns beside lakes where it is now impossible to buy a canoe made out of wood. But there are still people who want wooden canoes and who find people who make them, slowly, one at a time. Purists say wood handles better, that it is the right weight, heavy enough to steer a straight course, light enough to move quickly. Purists say the water makes a particular sound under it.

The novice canoeist cannot allow himself to be intimidated by tales of old canoes and old canoeists. If he cannot paddle for ten days without a break, he should not let that stop him from taking the canoe out tonight and enjoying what it can do. Canoes can sneak up on loons, and beavers and herons. Once discovered, the canoe does not terrify lake creatures. It has been a familiar sight for so long. In no particular hurry, the loon or the beaver ducks quietly under the water. The heron takes flight with its dignity intact, probably thinking: "It's only a canoe, but I'll just move away a bit anyway."

The canoe is a link with tradition; and the canoeist is too. There he is, his pipe in his mouth, all by himself on a lazy path, with no thought of Point A or Point B. Even now, when society has dictated that the pipe no longer be in the mouth, the sight is the same and the feeling inside the canoe is too. The lone canoeist can look around the lake, narrow his eyes a bit to block out the pastel cottages, and perhaps imagine an old boathouse or two where none exists now – and when he does that, he is his father or even his grandfather. He sits the same way in the canoe. In the canoe, his posture is better than it is on land. And his stroke is the same.

His stroke is a trick, passed down through the generations on lake after lake. He can make the canoe go straight ahead without changing sides with his paddle. He can paddle on the left side and make the canoe turn to the left. It is a simple trick, the J-stroke, but once he learns it, he links with his grandfather in his grandfather's canoe. He belongs in the canoe.

The J-stroke is the secret handshake of the old lake. Those who know it feel they have earned the right to disapprove of more modern pursuits – activities that take place at greater speed and make more noise. In the height of their disapproval, they watch the canoe races at the regatta on the long weekend, hopeful that the canoe will survive, hopeful that the racers will learn, in time, the thrill of slowing down.

The sight of a canoe is the sight of the past. It is the lake the way it used to be, before 300-horsepower motors were invented, before cottages were painted pastel. Long after the speedboaters have packed it in for the summer and gone back to their twenty-seven-speed bicycles, the canoeists are on the lake, taking their time, watching the leaves turn, and chatting to each other as they pass.

Sex

The Beast with Two Backs and Three Spider Bites

Cottage walls are thin and don't always go up to the ceiling. Cottage beds are not –

Put it this way: not enough attention is paid to cottage beds. They are not used the whole year, and if they are a bit lumpy hardly anyone notices. Cottagers are so tired when they go to bed, what with all the sun, that they crash instantly, without giving a thought to lumps, creaks –

Or narrowness. Cottage double beds were made before the United Nations-sanctioned standards for double bed sizes were ratified at The Hague, or perhaps it was Geneva. At any rate, either cottage beds were not mentioned or they were specifically exempted. Consequently, cottage double beds are narrower than their city counterparts. And they sag in the middle, unless they sag away from the middle and –

And inevitably they have one leg that is just a bit shorter than the others. When there is movement in the bed, such as when a person rolls over, or a person rolls under, the shorter leg bumps on the floor.

When you add it all up, you discover why sex at the cottage is –

Well, different, is what it is. Here you have men and women

cavorting about all day in the out-of-doors, eating well, getting exercise, feeling healthy. Or, if they are not doing that, at least feeling that they are. The cares of the city are behind them, they are at ease, they are relaxed, and what could be more conducive to a bit of the old one-two, or even the old eight-nine? But –

There is the question of the bed. It squeaks, and the short leg bumps. And the walls are thin and don't go all the way up to the ceiling. And there are people around, at close quarters, so –

So sex at the cottage tends to be a rather muffled activity. Groans and cries are stifled, in the interests of decency and good taste. But there is no stopping the short leg from bumping. That is why –

Sex at the cottage sounds like the approach of a short-of-breath person with a wooden leg.

Many is the child who has been frightened by it. Many the adult too. Many the participant, when you come right down to it. These muffled noises, these squeaks, these catchings of breath, these shushing sounds, these bumping sounds.

Not everyone thinks to complain, mind you. Those who have the best rooms are able to lie back afterwards and see the moon shimmering on the lake and be at peace. Nothing is more romantic.

This is assuming, however, that they have their nightshirts back on. Otherwise, the mosquitoes will get them or, while they sleep, the spiders. Experienced cottage lovers–that is, lovers *at* the cottage, as opposed to lovers *of* the cottage–know the perils. They are aware that prolonged nakedness, to coin a phrase, is an invitation to nocturnal biting species. Hence, experienced cottage lovers get back into their sleeping clothes as soon as is expedient. The more considerate of them will say: "That was nice," or something equally tender, first.

Then, reclothed, they will fall asleep in each others' arms – or away from each others' arms, depending on how the bed slopes.

❋ ❋ ❋

Cottage morality is a shifting thing, like the sands, although less cottage immorality takes place on the sands than you would think. The shifting quality of sand is not its only drawback.

It was not long ago that separate bedrooms for unmarried couples were the rule, and an unbending rule at that. It was fun, in those days, to watch the nephew and his fiancée try to catch a moment together, perhaps sneaking off for a time, to return covered in moss, or, if they were less knowledgeable, sand. It was even more fun if it was generally known that the nephew and the fiancée shared quarters in the city and were pretending, for the benefit of the family, to have met only long enough to have become engaged.

Nothing increases the ardour of a nephew and his fiancée more than soft breezes, the moon, and a wall between them. And, being less experienced in these matters, the nephew and his fiancée are, more often than not, going to challenge the barriers that keep them apart. Being less experienced in these matters, the nephew and his fiancée are not going to know about the mosquitoes. Nor are they going to know about the thin walls and the short leg on the bed. The sound of the short-of-breath one-legged person is going to be heard in the night, and the sound of suppressed giggles is going to be heard at the breakfast table the next day when the fiancée complains about spider bites.

It is at moments such as these that people who thought they were lovers discover new things about themselves – such as the absence of a sense of humour. If they are lucky enough to have their love survive and find one thing leading to another, they can experience the joy of returning to the cottage, with children, and trying to hide from them, for romantic purposes.

Since the children often, in their early years, sleep in the same room, this is not easy, although it is possible to pretend, up to a certain age, that the children do not know what is going on. Even below that certain age, children are impressionable and can hear a wooden-legged person approaching from miles away.

Later on, when the children are older and more likely to sleep longer, furtive activity is possible, always keeping in mind that in the event of discovery, the official story is: "Mommy and Daddy are playing."

The difficulty with such an official story is that it only works once. The second time, an alert child wants to know what Mommy and Daddy are playing and who's winning. A sufficiently imaginative answer will intrigue the children and cause them to inform everyone at the cottage that a game was being played.

It will also cause them to demand, every morning, that the game be played again.

This is why, eventually, all mommies and daddies must from time to time drop out of sight, and reappear, scratching, with bits of moss clinging to their clothing.

Interlude

The Long Weekend

Interlude

The Long Weekend
Two-Days-and-a-Bit of Desperate Fun

The long-weekend people differ from the all-summer people in easily identifiable ways. They talk louder and drive faster. They start laughing before they leave the car, and start drinking before they leave the marina.

Time is of the essence.

Long weekends may have been invented by banks. Certainly the concept of the long weekend as a bank holiday suggests that. It has been a few years since the phrase *bank holiday* has been used all that much, so it is difficult to remember if the bank holiday was intended to be a holiday for the bank or a holiday *from* the bank. Either way, the bank is closed, although the term has gone out of fashion.

Long weekend is the phrase now. Long weekends break up the summer. There is one in July and one in August. There is also one in September, but it is not thought of as belonging to the summer. It is thought of as belonging to the new school year.

After long weekends were invented by banks, they were legitimized by governments, which hate having holidays fall on Wednesdays and Tuesdays, which they would if governments just said something straightforward, like the bank holiday will fall on the 16th of August all the time. To avoid that, governments made complicated laws about when long weekends would fall. Most of us understand them, but occasionally someone comes back to work on the Tuesday, after everyone else has come back on Monday. And occasionally someone doesn't show up to work on the 16th of August.

But the concept of the long weekend is second nature to most of us now. Everybody knows it is coming, everybody knows it is time to get out of the city and down to the lake, and everybody knows that everybody else knows that. This means that getting to the lake will be an ordeal and it had bloody well better be fun once people get there. All the more so since it will be an ordeal getting *back* to the city too.

So there is a tinge of desperation to the long weekend that makes it unlike the rest of the summer. Summers are supposed to be lazy. People move slowly around, lie in the sun, paddle about in the water, turn the page. They eat when they feel like it and go to bed early. If it doesn't get done today, whatever it was, it will get done tomorrow. The thought applies to play as well as to work.

Except on the long weekend, when cars come screeching into the parking lot and desperate-looking people emerge, desperately laughing and checking their watches to see how many hours of fun are left. Everything but fun is a waste of time. Getting out of their clothes before they begin waterskiing is a waste of time. So is unpacking. So is turning down the music.

The lake comes alive and stays alive well into the night, well into the next morning, and well into the morning after that, and the one after that. Waterskiers buzz about, waving at something. Windsurfers jam the bay by the marina. Motorboats go around and around in circles. Houseboats try to go around and around in circles and bump into each other.

On Saturday and Sunday, Sports Day is going on at the yacht club. The organizers are feverishly organizing. Children are paddling, swimming, sailing, running, falling, and fighting. Their mothers and fathers are telling them what fun they are having. Some of the children are, in fact, having fun. Some of the children who aren't winning are even having fun.

Two of the organizers are in an argument over the rules of the three-legged race. Someone has been sent for a rulebook. A rulebook will be found, but there will be nothing in it about three-legged races. The contestants wait patiently, three-leggedly, for the argument to be settled. They have been promised trophies.

There is another argument about whether the wind is too strong for the sailing. One organizer is saying that wind is what sailing is supposed to be about. Another is worrying about the insurance.

Even in the wind, a swimming race for older people is going on. The older people, some as old as forty-five and resentful of being in a category called "Masters," have been very good about not cheering their children too hard in their races, not being pushy, not setting a bad example. Now they're in this Masters thing and they *really* want to win. But they can't show it. They have to win, while at the same time pretending they are not really trying all that hard. The children, not recognizing the complex emotions laid out before them, laugh.

Up the lake somewhere, a guy is running his annual barbecue for sixty-five people. It used to be an annual barbecue for twenty-five people, but it just grew, what with one thing and another. He roasts things on spits, which he has to turn himself, slowly, so as not to ruin the lamb and send sixty-five people home unhappy. Everyone thinks he loves turning the spit, everyone thinks it's an important tradition that he, and not someone else, turn the spit for several hours. No one knows that he has hated it for years. He may not know it himself, since he cannot imagine a long weekend without it. Every once in a while, someone brings him a beer, because it is hot work turning the spit, even in the rain.

Across the lake from that, the annual fireworks display is being prepared at the cottage where the annual fireworks display is always held. The fireworks are expensive now, and the hosts of the annual fireworks display have become so safety-conscious about the whole thing that rain seems like a good idea to them. So closely do they scrutinize the ground upon which the rockets are lit that they cannot even spare the time to look up in the sky and watch the patterns the big ones make. They have to make sure nothing is burning on the ground, and they have to make sure there is no repeat of that awful thing that happened in '83, when something made an awful bang in the purse of that lawyer's wife who was visiting from the city. Somehow the annual fireworks display hasn't seemed like quite so much fun since it became necessary for the hosts to take out insurance, but they continue with it anyway, for what would the long weekend be without it?

Somewhere the rule was written that an extra day added onto the weekend means fun must be had. There is no subsection ruling that people must move rapidly about in boats, cars, and other contraptions to have fun. But the fun-seeker knows: if he is not having fun where he is, he had better get somewhere else in a hurry. Much of the long weekend is spent going from where fun isn't to where fun is, then arriving there and finding out that fun just left and went somewhere else.

A lot of scurrying about results, frightening the animals, sending the fish into deeper water, and causing members of older generations to invent stories about the much more wholesome times they had when it was Bank Holiday Weekend and they were growing up.

Many of these stories are total fabrications involving collecting photographs of members of the royal family, listening to something on the wireless, and setting off tiny firecrackers that made so little noise they hardly disturbed anyone. The great thing about being a member of an older generation, particularly the oldest one, is that there are no older-still generations to correct your stories. Some of your contemporaries may quibble with you a bit on the details, but they have as much at stake in the basic theme as you do, the theme being that this generation can't hold a candle to previous ones.

Why, previous ones really *did* have to hold a candle. Did you know . . .

Then it starts up again, another reminiscence, causing an unexpected lull in the long weekend festivities and inciting a string of other reminiscences by members of other generations, for some of whom the good old days were about five years ago. It is a wonder that anyone can party at all, what with all the chatter about better parties.

Further obstacles to partying are often posed by the hosts of long-weekenders. The problem is one of metabolism. The hosts, if they have been at the lake a while, have slowed down. Their heartbeats are where Nature intended them to be. They have stopped wearing watches. They have stopped reading newspapers, or at least the front sections. They keep the radio off. If dinner is late, they don't care. In fact, they don't know, because dinner doesn't have to be at any particular time, since nothing is happening after it.

Some of them have stopped swearing and talking about real estate.

Into this sluggish world come frantic fun-seekers, wearing digital watches, conscious, to the minute, of the allotted time remaining. Their cry is: "What'll we do now?" Their fear is that the beer will run out. Their second fear is that the sun won't shine. With only two days and a bit to enjoy, they lack the wisdom to see that Nature put rainy days on Earth so that people could stop sun-tanning, stop charging around in boats, stop trying to finish staining the deck and instead lie down with a book and perhaps even have a nap.

If the sun doesn't shine, the long-weekend people take it as a personal affront and a gyp. They worked hard to get down here, fought the traffic. And now look. And what are the all-summer people doing? Sleeping. Reading a book. Talking. About birds. Not even looking at the sky to see when it will clear.

The what'll-we-do-now people may be, in other times and other places, very close to the other people, the what-does-it-matter people. But in the same place on a long weekend, they are not going to get along. The blood is not coursing through their veins at the same speed. One has adrenalin, the other doesn't. One is looking ahead to Saturday night, the other doesn't know which night it is. One is worrying, almost from the time of arrival, about going back to the city. For the other, the city is only a dim memory.

The two sides tire of each other easily. All over the lake the two sides are getting tired of each other. Wiser souls among them know that next year the roles may be reversed. Today's contented and snail-paced cottagers may be next summer's desperate three-day hedonists. But for today and tomorrow and about half of Monday, the conflict will continue.

Then, finally, there will be cheery waves at the dock, assurances that a wonderful time was had, the sound of automobile engines, and it will be over, until the next one, a month or a year down the road. The lake returns to normal. A minute ago it looked like a beer commercial, awash with grinning people, laughing and shouting. Now it looks like a body of water with a couple of small boats on it.

Quiet returns. The animals return. The fish come back. The sun comes out.

Part 5

Cottage Creatures

Loons

A Canadian Success Story

Everybody talks about the cry of the loon – *now*. The cottage would not be the same without the loon, everybody says. Without the loon, an essential element of the nation's heritage – the *world's* heritage – would vanish. A lot of fuss is made over loons, their call, their habitat, their survival.

It was not always this way. For years, the loon laboured away in anonymity, providing background noise for hammocks, campfires, and canoes. No one much noticed. Praise was reserved for mallards, Canada geese, and other birds that could fly in formation. If anybody paid any attention to the loon at all, it was to notice that it seemed to take rather a long time for it to get up in the air. And if anybody paid any attention beyond that, it was to remark that loons, on occasion, completely lost their dignity, flapping around clumsily in the water and making silly sounds.

As a bird, the loon did not seem to belong in Canada. Canadians were more reserved. They did not flap around clumsily and make silly sounds, and were not about to waste their valuable time taking notice of a bird that did. This was years before the televising of Parliament.

At the cottage, people trained their high-powered binoculars on tiny birds and spent precious hours trying to tell whether they (the birds) were male or female, while loons wailed away in the distance and performed much as they do today, completely neglected by people. Cottage Man neither knew nor cared that the loon was capable of floating three different ways.

The loon's ignored period, painful as it must have been, was followed by one even worse – the period of mocking and ridicule. Loons were made fun of, their names, on popular television shows, made synonymous with craziness. "Loon," when people looked it up in the dictionary, meant not only a diving bird but a worthless, sorry, lazy, or stupid fellow, from a Scandinavian word meaning "base conduct." An old adjective gained a new currency: loony. There were no adjectives for mallards or Canada geese, no mallardy or geesey. So current did the adjective become that it became a noun: a loony. So prevalent did the use of noun and adjective become that a debate arose as to the spelling of it. Loony or looney or loonie?

Through it all, the loon sailed, sometimes calmly, sometimes not, o'er the lakes, taking flight, with difficulty, always calling, sometimes even seeming to laugh. Unaware that the various calls of the loon would one day be regarded as sacred, scornful cottagers yelled at it from their docks. They insulted it, calling it a loon. "Shut up, you loon!" they yelled.

Nobody cared that the loon had survived 60 million years, which was much longer than any cottager had. Nobody cared that the loon had red eyes and could live up to thirty years. It didn't bother anybody that loons needed a running start and could not take off on land, which meant that if they happened to land in a puddle, it was game over. Loons were silly, was all anybody thought about them.

The change in the loon's status, from figure of ridicule to honoured symbol, came almost overnight. No one is sure when or why. But all of a sudden, the loon was on the dollar coin. True, no one liked the dollar coin all that much, but being on it provided a much-needed ego boost for the loon. There is nothing like being on a coin to make you feel better about yourself.

After the coin came coffee-table books about loons. Coffee-table books are usually reserved for dead painters and the landscapes of European countries, so it was no small achievement for the loon to appear on one. Loon lore began to figure in cottage chit-chat. Everybody now knew that loons had solid bones and had no direct evolutionary relationship with grebes.

There was no stopping the loon after that. It became the official bird of Ontario. People made speeches about it, praising its many fine attributes, such as mating for life and being silent in winter. Record albums were next, featuring the wide range of noises of which the loon was capable. Debate arose as to whether a particular call was the well-known tremolo, made in flight, or the famous territorial yodel. Fist fights broke out in bars near lakes. The promise of loon calls began to feature in cottage real estate ads. Loon calendars appeared at Christmas.

As matters now stand, the loon is regarded as a distinguished citizen of cottage country. While some worry about its going Hollywood, it continues to behave much as it always has, flying with its head lower than its body, floating either in the up, medium, or down positions, and emitting any of its four distinctive cries, upon hearing which, children turn to their parents and say: "That sounds just like the record!"

Tourists

There Goes the Neighbourhood

Cottagers think they are known in the towns and villages where they do their shopping and stow their boats, but they are not. In the eyes of the townspeople and villagers – the year-rounders – the cottagers are summer people, around for two, three, or four weeks at a time, or maybe just weekends. Not too many locals can memorize a face or a name in that period of time. That is the objective reality. But reality does not exist in the heart of the cottager. As far as the cottager is concerned, he is almost a full-time resident, an old-timer with roots in the community. After all, he's been coming here for years, and his family before that.

To him, that means he's not to blame for all the traffic, all the noise, all the illegal parking. It's the tourists who do that. The tourists just pass through. They don't spend three weeks at a time in the community. They have no long-term commitment to it.

But, say the cottagers, when they meet each other at parties, at the yacht club, at the cottage owners' association, it's sure going downhill, isn't it? Those tourists come through with their trailers, their campers, their cars with stickers from Disneyland and some caverns in Idaho plastered on the back. They demand

souvenirs and souvlaki. They ride the tour boats and throw
plastic cups in the water. They rent houseboats and play loud
music fifty yards from the cottage dock. They take pictures,
mostly of each other.

The war between the cottagers and the tourists would be
more interesting if the tourists knew it was on. The war between
the cottagers and the tourists would be like the war between
the sheepherders and the cattlemen. There would be attacks and
counterattacks, pine cones lobbed at trailers, empty soft-drink
cans hurled at outhouses. But the tourists don't know they're
in a war. They just pass through town, look for a place to wash
up, fill up the propane tank, grab a postcard, take a few snaps,
buy some more film, and they are off, with bad will towards
none.

The cottager, on the other hand, is deeply resentful. He is
deeply resentful because the tourist, fly-by-night creature though
he may be, is taken seriously in the community. Despite his silly
shirts and Ontario Place hat, he has more economic clout than
the cottager. The town economy is shifting. There are fewer
stores for the cottager, more stores for the tourist. There is only
one hardware store left; there are twenty boutiques. There are
fewer places to buy kerosene, more places to buy a satin Elvis
pillow, a plastic imitation of an Eskimo carving, and a miniature
bottle of maple syrup that doesn't exactly, when you look at it,
come from this particular town, or this exact province, actually,
but from a province not too far away.

The locals, the townspeople, seem all too willing to sell this
stuff, all too reluctant to keep the needs of the cottage, such as
a certain grade of black screening, in stock. Insufficiently grateful
for the continued custom of the cottagers, the townspeople
allow the waterfront to be populated by outdoor cafés and
antique stores, forcing the cottager to go to the highway for a
shear pin, or to the shopping centre for a fishing line.

The town is always throwing some sort of shindig for the
tourists. Pickerel Days, for example, where there is a quilting
bee during the daytime and a big street dance at night, and

people with out-of-province licence plates get to park free. Whereas the cottagers, if they leave their cars behind the ball diamond overnight, are always getting tickets and notes warning that they will be towed away.

Of course, the tourists are not aware of any of this. They breeze into town, park at a free spot, check out the Pickerel Days display, and rent, by the hour, a little yellow boat they can pedal. They have a pleasant time, going at about one and a half miles per hour. Then when they round a corner and look out from under the awning of the pedal boat, they can't understand why those people on that dock are glaring at them.

"Typical tourists," the cottagers on the dock are thinking, although the tourists are not doing anything in particular, other than pedalling a yellow boat with an awning on it. Furthermore, they have not done anything typical, as far as they know, and have no intention of doing anything typical in the foreseeable future.

Unaware of the resentment they are causing, the tourists will pedal back to the marina and, before they drive to the next town, buy some postcards with typical scenes, in order to let the folks back home know about Pickerel Days, and that they never saw a pickerel during them.

Americans

They Probably Don't Mean Any Harm

Scene in the Loblaws, the Steinberg's, or the IGA: Two young men are laughing. One of them is holding up a can of coffee. "I bet this is pretty hot stuff," he says, and the other one laughs. Others in the store look at each other and nod. Americans. In all the world, only Americans think it is unusual, quaint, and funny that other countries have their own brand names.

This isn't to suggest that Americans mean any harm. It's just the way they are. Later, they will tell you what good coffee it is and invite you in for a cup, after they have made sure that you folks drink coffee up here.

Some cottagers are offended by such behaviour and take out their resentment by being mean to tourists. It is a mistake to do so. All Americans are tourists, but not all tourists are Americans. It is worth remembering that and not waste your most toadying manner, or your loftiest nationalism, on somebody from Vancouver, just because he is wearing $200 running shoes and whistling something from *Cats*.

Not too many years ago, you could always spot an American at the lake. An American was rich, arrogant, loud, and ignorant. His car was too big and so was his boat. His clothes were bright and his questions weren't. He had the latest in equipment – fishing rods that folded up so that they would fit in the glove compartment, at least the glove compartment of *his* car; chairs that swivelled in the boat; electronic gear that beeped and pinged to measure the depth of the water and ascertain the presence of fish. The American had too much money and too few manners. You could always tell.

Nowadays it is harder. Progress and prosperity have come to our country, with the result that many Canadians now fit the same description. Unless a tourist is carrying a gun, it is next to impossible to tell if he is an American, without a good look at the licence plates. But there are some tell-tale signs:

1. An American knows the rules. He has studied up on the lake and knows what the cost of a fishing licence is, what the limits are, and when the season ends. No cottager has ever possessed such information.

2. An American is pleasant, generous, and friendly. His Canadian counterpart is careful with his money and suspicious of strangers. The American will invite you on board his boat and show it off to you. He will tell you that it was meant to be an ocean-going boat, which is why it has the five bedrooms and the dance floor, but he decided to tootle around some of these lakes with it first.

3. An American, while not suspicious of strangers, is suspicious of foreign brand names. He suspects the coffee may not really be coffee; he brings his own supply of cigarettes and scotch; he and his wife spend some time at the supermarket discussing whether Canadian J-cloths will really do the job.

4. An American is always afraid that someone will speak French to him.

5. An American is very proud of his home town and, regardless of the magnificence of the scenery around him, will stop to show a Canadian pictures of it. After the American brags about his home town, the Canadian will brag about his trip to New York.

It is only recently that Americans have begun to travel widely, and their experiences in foreign lands have been limited, but extreme. They have had foreigners cheering at them and strewing roses in their path. They have had foreigners shooting at them. They have had foreigners sneering at them and over-charging them in restaurants. What they encounter in your cottage community may fit into none of these categories of experience, so it is wise to be patient with them while they get their bearings and accustom themselves to the native coffee. In a day or so, they will be gone, because they have limited time and want to hit as many lakes as possible.

Bats

A Friend Perched on the Outhouse Wall

Bat scholars – kind, thoughtful people with their hearts in the right places – have written of Our Friend the Bat. Minding his own business all during the daylight hours, Our Friend comes out of hiding at dusk and eats up thousands of mosquitoes that would otherwise eat up us. Then Our Friend goes quietly back to his Bat House and minds his own business, leaving us to enjoy a bug-free evening.

This is in theory. Since, in practice, bug-free evenings are few and far between, the conclusion can be drawn that there are too few bats, rather than too many.

It is true, the kind, thoughtful people will admit, that Our Friend sometimes builds his Bat House in between the walls of structures that we thought were ours. And it is true, bat scholars further agree, that Our Friend and his Friends are wont to squeak a bit once at home, the squeaking being clearly audible to humans on the other side of the wall. As we know, humans set extremely high standards for themselves and their friends. High standards often make it difficult for humans to recognize that they too would squeak a little if they had just consumed half their body weight in mosquitoes.

Bat scholars know all this, and they also know that it is erroneous to worry about bats flying into your face and flapping their wings in your nose and getting stuck in your hair, squeaking in desperation to get free, thus summoning hundreds of other bats to help out. Bat scholars know there is nothing to this. Bats can see very well, much better than humans can at certain times of day – specifically the time when it is too dark to see a bat coming but too bright for the street lamps to come on, assuming that there are some around the cottage, which there probably aren't.

Bats can see absolutely perfectly at such times because they have radar or sonar or something. Fortunately for bats, the sonar or radar or something is built right in and does not have to be carried around, weighing Our Friend down. With sonar or radar, Our Friend can avoid you, even when you, not seeing too well and wishing there were street lamps, reach up and try to catch him with your hand, thinking he's a Frisbee someone has tossed at you.

Still another reason not to worry about Our Friend the Bat is that he's not a vampire. Contrary to popular mythology, a vampire bat does not wear a cape and say "Good evening!" when you least expect it. A vampire bat is merely a bat that feeds on blood, has razor-sharp teeth that cut into its prey, and an anti-coagulant in its saliva that keeps the enemy's blood from clotting. "These bats do not occur in Canada," says the encyclopaedia.

That is one of the most popular features of Canadian bats and may help to counterbalance the fact that their droppings are no nicer than anyone else's and have the added disadvantage of being hard to locate. There was a cottage on an island where the oldest aunt always said: "Out of sight, out of mind." After only half a summer with bats she began saying it less frequently.

To sum up, then: The Canadian bat has bad toilet habits and squeaks between the walls, but he is not a vampire and will not fly into your nose in the dark. Plus he eats, on a daily basis,

50 per cent of his body weight in insects. Truly, he is Our Friend the Bat.

❋ ❋ ❋

This being said, there are times when it is more difficult to accept the notion, such as when one is seated in the outhouse and notices that, perched on the wall beside him, is Our Friend.

This really happened at a cottage up north. Unfortunately, some time elapsed before the discovery was made, according to the man–not a bat scholar–who made it. "If I had seen it there, I think I would have used the woods," the man said.

However, Our Friend, because it was a Canadian bat, did not say "Good evening!" or in any other way call attention to itself. And because it was dark in the outhouse and there were no street lamps, the bat escaped discovery until the man was seated and concentrating on things other than what might be perched on the wall beside him.

"There was this thing on the wall," he said, after he had fully recovered from the experience. "I thought it was something dead, or a lump of mud. I poked at it with my flashlight and it looked at me."

Seen close up, Our Friend is small and a bit like a mouse. It is also a lot like a bat. The man, possessed of a logical and orderly mind, faced several choices, none of which he liked much.

"One: I could yell for help," he said. "Then a dozen people would come running and see me, a grown man, sitting there trembling, with my pants around my ankles.

"Two: I could ignore it. But I wasn't sure it would ignore me. I mean, I knew there had never been a vampire bat in North America. But it would only take one, wouldn't it?

"Three: I could run. But I wasn't in a good position to run.

"Four: I could try to make the bat move. But where was it going to go? It might fly up into my face and flap its wings in my nose. Also, how was I going to move it? I could yell, but what would I yell? 'Shoo, bat!'? I'd feel silly yelling something like that. And everybody would come running and ask what I was yelling at. And I would have to yell through the closed doors that I was yelling 'Shoo, bat!' and there would be a big discussion through the outhouse door about whether you could yell 'shoo' at bats or whether that was only for cats. Everybody would argue about it and I'd be sitting there in the outhouse trying not to disturb the bat any more than it was already disturbed. And finally someone would arrive late, find out I was yelling at a bat and say: 'Don't be silly. The bat is Our Friend.'

"Five: I could try to dislodge it with something like a long stick, but this outhouse didn't have a long stick in it. It just never occurred to anyone that a long stick would come in handy in an outhouse. Something like a plunger would have been good. But plungers go with running water and outhouses don't have any.

"There was no long stick, just my flashlight. It wasn't a very long flashlight. I didn't want to touch the bat with it. Even if it didn't fly up and flap its wings in my nose and even if it didn't bite my neck, it would still be flying around in there in the dark and its sonar could go wrong and it could crash into me. I liked the bat better just sitting there.

"If I opened the door and dislodged the bat, maybe the bat would fly out the door. But somebody might be outside. I mean, we all know each other pretty well here, but still . . .

"I sat there and thought about it a while. I had more or less forgotten what I'd gone there for in the first place. The bat was still there, looking at me. I decided to open the door just a bit and use the flashlight. I took a deep breath and nudged the bat with it. The bat didn't move. I nudged it a little harder. The bat took two steps to the left and stopped. It looked at me. I reached for it with the flashlight again. I thought about hitting it. Then I thought about cleaning off the flashlight.

"Suddenly the bat flew out the door. Maybe it thought about me hitting it about the same time as I did. I left as quickly as I could, not feeling any more kindly towards bats than I ever did. When I was back inside the cottage I tried to tell them

about the bat being in the outhouse. They were in the middle
of a card game and wouldn't look up.

" 'Guess what I saw in the outhouse,' I said.

" 'Two hearts,' my brother said.

" 'A bat,' I said.

" 'That's gross,' my niece said.

" 'Two spades,' my wife said.

" 'Don't talk about it,' my younger aunt said.

"I said it was right on the wall and everybody said don't
talk about it, except for my niece who said:

" 'Where did it go?'

" 'I don't know,' I said.

" 'Out of sight, out of mind,' my older aunt said."

❉   ❉   ❉

There was an island down the lake where they didn't have as
much patience with bats. Every evening for a couple of weeks
twenty or thirty bats would come flying out from under the
roof somewhere and about half a dozen of them, instead of
flying up the hill and out over the lake and wherever they usually
went, would fly around the veranda and even into the main
house.

There was a lot of concern about the older people when
that happened. Of course, the older people weren't among those
who were worried. The older people had seen a lot of bats in
their day and hadn't seen very many vampire movies. What
worried the older people was all the younger people running
through the veranda and into the main house with badminton
racquets and flashlights and shouting "There he goes!" and "Hit
him!" and "Don't worry, Grandma!"

The dogs enjoyed the action and began looking forward to
it. They took to chasing each other through the veranda and
into the main house, barking loudly, even when a bat hadn't
been spotted. In the excitement, a couple of the children bumped
into things and fell down, for which the bats were held responsible. It was Man Against the Wilderness, the way some of them

on the island began to see it, Us Against Them. And the older islanders gradually came to agree because they were tired of people running through the living room at dusk with badminton racquets.

It didn't help matters, as far as Our Friends were concerned, that mosquito activity was at its height. All day long the mosquitoes were biting, and especially at dusk, just at about the time the bats were supposed to be dining (or was it breakfasting) on them. This enabled the militants amongst the island's population to deflect the Our Friends Hypothesis, as it had come to be known.

"If the bat is Our Friend," the militants said, "how come there are mosquitoes all over my neck?"

Ironically, the mosquito, archenemy and sometime meal of the bat, became the engine of its undoing on this particular island. Despairing of the bats ever functioning effectively as insect eliminators, the islanders decided to fog the mosquito-ridden vicinity with a commercial gadget operating on the same principle as a flame-thrower. In the middle of the fogging operation, the wind shifted, filling the eaves of the main house with oily vapours and sending the bats into a panic. Out they came, in broad daylight, one by one, through a hole in the wall.

The militants had an idea. After gaining the consent of their fellow campers through exaggerated tales of vampires, rabies, and increasingly deeper-voiced squeaks from between the walls, the militants improvised a deadly welcome for the emerging bats. It consisted of a section of screening, loosely rolled into a funnel, with a large plastic bag fastened to one end with masking tape. The open end of the funnel, called the Bat Slide, was fastened to the opening in the wall. Bats would, so the theory went, emerge from the hole in the wall when mosquito fogging commenced, and fly out, only to find themselves surrounded by window screening. Trying to put on the brakes, they would skid into the plastic bag, which was dubbed the Bat Trap.

Seven people were required to put this plan into action. One worked the fogger. One stood on a kitchen chair and held the Bat Slide to the hole in the wall. One held the kitchen chair. One made sure the Bat Slide was securely attached to the Bat Trap. One looked up under the eavestroughing and said: "I think I hear them coming." Another ran in and out of the main house keeping the people inside informed, since most of them were afraid of bats or didn't want to watch for one reason or another.

The seventh person on the team stood about fifteen feet away, held a flashlight, and said: "I'm not sure we should be doing this."

The members of this particular group, the story goes, had worked together on many other projects before, and only one thing could have surprised them. As luck would have it, the one thing that could have surprised them did: the Bat Slide and the Bat Trap worked like a charm.

Bat after bat emerged from the hole in the wall just under the eavestrough. Bat after bat took flight, then – too late – tried to stop, only to slide down a plastic wall. As the news of this triumph was relayed to the islanders inside the main house, more and more of them stepped outside to look until, eventually, there were five people saying: "I'm not sure we should be doing this" and three people holding the bag.

The bag was full of bats, and this is what no one had anticipated. Because no one had expected the scheme to work, no one had thought about what you do with a bag full of live bats. In theory, the folks on the island up the lake had the bats where they wanted them, but now, having them where they wanted them, they didn't want them any more.

What do you do with a bag of live bats? As they pondered their options, they discovered there were not many. They could, one person said – the person who first said "I'm not sure we should be doing this" – drop the bag and run away. But where would they run away to, particularly since they were just outside the back door?

They could throw the bag as far as they could and let the bats fly away. But the bats would only come back.

They could tie the top of the bag and throw it as far as they could. But that would lead, eventually, to a bag full of dead bats, and while this alternative was attractive to the militants, it made the children say "Awwwww!" and look mournful and it made one of the aunts say: "I *told* you!"–although no one could remember her telling anybody anything.

Saying "Shoo, bats!" was out of the question.

It was almost dark. They could, one of the children suggested, let the bats go, but not before speaking sternly to them and saying let this be a lesson to them: this is what happened to bats that refused to stay out of the veranda and even flew into the main house and bothered the older people. The child abandoned this plan after it was suggested to him that he hold the bag open while the bats flew out.

Another of the children had a more colourful idea: they could take the bats out in the boat, maybe drive for five minutes out onto the lake in the dark and then throw the bag into the water.

Then what? somebody asked.

Then the bats would drown.

"Awwww!" the younger children said, and some of their mothers too.

What if they got away? one of the militants asked.

They wouldn't know where they were and would fly to another island.

No, said one of the militants. They'd fly right back here. Better to tie up the bag and throw it into the water and let it sink.

"Awwwww!" the children said, except for the one who had proposed the original idea and wanted desperately to go on a boat ride in the dark. That child, a small girl, asked: "What if it doesn't sink?"

There was a silence, during which a deep masculine voice could be heard muttering: "I'm not sure we should be doing this." Then the little girl answered her own question. "We take some great big rocks, see, and we drop them on top of the bag of bats until it sinks."

A hush greeted this suggestion, broken only by the sound of what might have been bat wings brushing against the inside of a plastic bag. Then several childlike voices could be heard in the dark asking if they could come along and watch. Three of the men conferred quietly, out of earshot of the rest. Then they set off down the path with the bag of bats.

It was dark and none of them had ever walked along a darkened path with a bag of live bats before. There was no precedent for it, one of them thought. Anything could happen. Another thought he heard a voice say "Good evening!" But he kept it to himself.

At the other end of the island they put the bag down, opened it and ran away from it. When they were sure they had not been followed they stopped to confer.

"I can't believe that worked," one said.

"I know," the second replied.

"Oh well," said the third.

"After all," said the first.

"I know," said the second. "The bat is Our Friend."

"Oh well," said the third, and they walked back to the main house in the dark, slapping at their necks where the mosquitoes were biting.

Friends

Sophistication Counts for Nothing in the Bush

People who have cottages and friends learn not to invite the latter to the former if they want them to remain the latter. The very qualities – sophistication, intellect, irony, and palate – that make for close friendships in the city are of little use when the plumbing is outdoors and the nearest four-star restaurant is hundreds of miles away.

It takes time, and many wasted weekends, to learn the lesson: Good company in the city counts for nothing in the bush.

The trouble begins with the arrival. The friends bring flowers – an insult to the beauty, nay, majesty, of their hosts' surroundings. Flowers are wrong. Chocolates are right. Wine could be all right, but is risky. Sometimes people decide to be healthy at the cottage. Being healthy at the cottage means you drink less wine and eat more chocolates. As presents, books are great, as long as they are not about making money.

If the presentation of the present does not worsen the situation, the first attempts at conversation probably will. The proper introductory cottage conversation is about how horrible the drive up was. Cottagers like that. It makes them feel good about where they are, the fact that they have already done that drive and will not have to do it again for a while. As a rule, any topic relating to how much city people are suffering is appropriate for cottage conversation.

The vicarious enjoyment of urban suffering does not, however, extend to gossip, to theories of possible marriage breakups among neighbours and mutual friends. People go to the cottage to get away from the troubles of their friends and to concentrate on their own. Also, they don't like to think that they are missing anything interesting back home. Similar reasoning applies to politics, in particular, and current events, in general. If cottage people are reading newspapers at all, it is only the sports pages or the weather forecast. They do not want to know about rumours of a new outbreak of rampant factionalism in the Liberal Party. They do not want to have new developments in Libya brought to their attention. They are likely to feel inferior when such topics are raised. Plus, they are not interested. They are interested in the state-of-the-art septic system, the sunset, the absence of raccoons, how hot it is in the city, and, once more, how bad the drive up was.

Guests can recover from the wrong gift and bad conversation by being what is known as "good campers." Many things go into making a good camper, but the primary one is this: A good camper never complains.

If his bed is more comfortable in the city, he does not say so. If the menu is less varied than he is used to, he bites his tongue. If the weather is too cold or too hot, if the water is nicer to swim in somewhere else, a good camper keeps these observations to himself.

Further:

A good camper does not need hot water.

A good camper brings clothes that are bad enough to paint in.

A good camper is not afraid of raccoons.

A good camper does the dishes and doesn't mention dishwashers.

A good camper is not afraid of toads.

A good camper does not talk while people are reading mysteries.

A good camper has a good recipe for stew and willingly cooks it, but doesn't talk about it.

A good camper never uses the word *quaint*.

A good camper plays Clue with the host's children.

A good camper doesn't pretend he can drive the boat.

A good camper knows when to stay with the group and when to go off alone.

✳   ✳   ✳

The last is the most difficult concept for rookie guests to learn. Stunned by the scenery, jangled by the drive, lured by the quiet, some guests immediately seek to take off by themselves, to be alone, to get away from it all. They grab a canoe or just head off down the path. The problem is that in getting away from it all they also get away from the people who invited them there. This is an inconsiderate act. The hosts need to be complimented on the setting (as if somehow they can take credit for it). They need the opportunity to brag a bit about the cottage and its surroundings, and the little touches they have added.

A sensitive guest recognizes all this and may also be aware of a deeper need – a need for reinforcement. His hosts need to be absolved of guilt for being here. Their unease at being out of the rat race must be taken away. They need to know that nothing much is going on in the city, that they are not falling behind in any area of work or life by staying out here. They need, once again, to be told how difficult the drive was and how hot it is in the city.

After a short period of what might be called debriefing, it is permissible for guests to disappear, after first inquiring about meal times.

Sleeping is the area in which mistakes by guests are most commonly made. Most guests know enough to go to bed when their hosts do, but not everyone understands the finer points of getting up. Some, rendered punchy by the fresh air and the sound of early-morning birds, arise at dawn and begin crashing around in the kitchen, whistling. Invariably, anyone that enthusiastic winds up breaking something. This will cause one of his hosts to arise much earlier than usual. If the host doesn't hear the sound of breakage, he will awaken eventually to the sound of his guest trying to find the broom.

The reverse mistake is to sleep in. Feeling, perhaps too acutely, the strains and pressures of the city, the guest decides he will catch up, over one weekend, on all the sleep he has been missing in the past three weeks. When he arrives at the table, just after lunch, and asks what's for breakfast, he will, if he is just slightly sensitive, realize something is wrong. If he is just a little bit more sensitive than that, he will not overcompensate by arising at dawn the next day and whistling. A good camper, by contrast, finds out when his hosts customarily arise. He then arises ten minutes earlier and, being very careful, makes the coffee.

The guests have been invited because their hosts want to see them. On the other hand, it is a good thing for guests to realize that their hosts undergo fundamental changes at the cottage. They become accustomed to a degree of solitude. They enjoy it, knowing it is fleeting. Nothing breaks the mood more easily than a jovial guest suddenly appearing and asking: "Well, what's on the agenda today?"

A good camper doesn't have an agenda.

The trick, when being a guest, is to keep a respectful distance from the hosts, smile often, and approach only when summoned.

The same principle applies to helping. Thinking, erroneously, that a good camper pitches in, rookie guests too often grab the nearest axe, hammer, or saw and go off looking for things to fix. Rookie guests have felled healthy trees and caused them to fall the wrong way, taking down power lines. Rookie guests have dropped key bolts in the water, they have sawed through three-inch nails, painted windows shut, spray-painted screens, and tossed into the fireplace a valuable and significant copy of the sports section of the *Toronto Star*.

A useful rule of thumb is that any task more complicated than sweeping, doing dishes, or carrying stuff up from the boat, should only be done after consultation. Furthermore, the rule on repairs is: don't call us, we'll call you.

Thus, an experienced guest camper stands close, but not too close, to the host while he works. Occasionally, the guest will ask if he can get anything. Occasionally, the host will say: "Could you hand me that wrench over there?"

Conversation is often permitted during these work periods, with the skilful guest saying things like "Looks like you've got it now" and the host saying things like "I think we're getting there."

Notice the use of *we*. The host doesn't want to hog the credit. In his mind, the task has been done jointly. "We did it," he will tell the others at the end of the day, even though the guest only fetched wrenches and, once, held a board steady.

But the guest made a contribution, by not doing all the other things he might have done on his own. When he takes leave of his hosts and they thank him for all his help, that may be what they mean.

Weeds

The Saga of the Good Scissors

The chicken wire experiment seemed, at the time, to work pretty well. Swimmers reported considerably fewer weeds. But it was an exhausting thing to do and it made you feel silly, marching backwards through the water, holding on to an end of chicken wire, while your family held on to the rest, dragging it along the bottom in the hope of pulling out weeds.

It turned out not to work so well. Within weeks, the weeds were back. Somebody, a teen-ager who was reading science fiction that summer, said there seemed to be more of them than there were before. The teen-ager said that the weeds might be angry about the chicken wire.

Still, it beat last year's method, which was to take a deep breath and surface-dive to the bottom, grab handfuls of weeds – trying to get them by the root – and pull them up. That was slow, and blotches appeared to be growing on your hands after a while, although they probably weren't. The same teen-ager who complained about the anger of the weeds after the chicken wire claimed there was the beginning of a rash on his left thumb that was not explainable in any rational way.

And why were you doing this, anyway? The weeds weren't

hurting anyone, you said, as *your* left thumb began suddenly to itch, possibly in sympathy.

"Well," it was explained to you, "they're unsightly."

Nature, you replied, had its unsightly moments. It was part of God's plan.

That, you were told, was the same excuse you used for not dragging the big dead tree off the path. God must be a pretty sloppy person.

You said no, God wasn't a sloppy person, but the weeds must be there for a reason.

"The reason," it was explained to you, "is to hide leeches and bloodsuckers and turtles and things that infect and bite you when you go swimming."

"Nonsense," you said. "God would never do that. I think God put the weeds there so the fish could hide and catch some little things to eat."

"I don't like swimming in fish," it was explained to you.

"Me neither," it was explained to you in a younger voice.

You tried to explain that if the fish did not have places to hide, the bigger fish would catch them and eat them up. Also the weeds were plants and plants put nutrients back into the air, or at least the water, you thought, by photosynthesizing or breathing and creating oxygen or carbon something, which was essential to our life here on earth.

"As long as it doesn't happen off our dock where people are swimming," said a big voice, in a reasonable but perhaps ominous way.

This was the time of the good scissors incident, the stainless steel ones winding up somehow at the bottom of the lake, where they may still be rusting, for all anyone knows, although there is disagreement as to whether stainless steel rusts at all, or whether things that are at the bottom of the lake rust while they are there or only when they are taken out.

As the good scissors cannot be found, no one can know for sure. They vanished after the experiment with the scythe failed badly. The scythe experiment was the first brave attempt to stave off chemical warfare against the weeds. The question had been raised by the purchasing of a plastic jug full of some guaranteed non-toxic chemical. The pro-chemical faction making the purchase had been assured that the chemical would hurt only the weeds, and even then not so much as to make them suffer.

But the anti-chemical faction, the same one whose left thumb had begun itching uncontrollably, put forward the position that chemicals should be used only as a last resort, and even then only as a last resort.

"And who wants to own a last resort?" the anti-chemical faction added, thinking humour might take some of the strain out of the situation.

It did not, and the anti-chemical faction tried a different tactic, which consisted of pleading. "The weeds may not be very nice," the anti-chemical faction said, "but at least we know who created them. Who knows who or *what* created this chemical?"

"You're using God again," it was explained to him.

"Only as a last resort," the anti-chemical faction replied. He then asked for time to try a new and vastly improved technique. This turned out to consist of diving into the water carrying a small hand-held scythe that would be used to cut the weeds.

The theory was all right. In practice, the attempt to swing the scythe underwater served only to spin the anti-chemical faction in circles. The circles were not harmful at all to the weeds but threatened to cause disorientation in the anti-chemical faction.

Surfacing, and seeing fingernails being drummed impatiently upon a plastic guaranteed non-toxic chemicals jug, the anti-chemicals faction began the process of losing the good scissors. Racing to the kitchen and grabbing them out of a drawer, he begged for one more chance.

Returning to the dock, he donned a diving mask and set to work. Dive after dive, snip after snip, he worked on the weeds, cutting quite a few and causing them to float to the surface. It was impressive-looking work, and only the anti-chemical faction knew how many weeds remained.

"I'm making great progress," he announced when it was time to go up for dinner. "Just give me five more minutes."

Later, he appeared at the table announcing that he had given up and had tried the chemicals. It was too soon to know how well they would work. In fact, the chemicals were stashed in the boathouse, under a tarpaulin. Subsequently, when large and small voices were raised at the dock, complaining about slimy weedy gunk and tentacles interfering with swimming and probably playing host to hundreds of awful weed-bed creatures, the anti-chemical faction could reply: "We've done everything we can, so let's stop worrying about it. What's a little weed? If the acid rain comes, there won't be any weeds at all. Will you like that?"

This kept the anti-weed forces silent until the next summer, by which time everyone had forgotten where the good scissors were.

Fiancées

The Moment of Truth

He was at the cottage for nine days and every morning they brought him breakfast in bed. It was only later that he realized it was because they hated him. By that time it was too late.

The woman was gone. She had moved him out of her life and moved on. It was because he was not a "good camper," he heard eventually. He didn't understand at first.

"How could I not be a good camper? I wasn't even camping. They gave me a room and I slept in it and her people seemed to like me well enough. They brought me breakfast in bed every morning."

Soon enough, he found out. A good camper fits in. He did not. This had been the big test. She had brought him to her cottage for two weeks, introduced him to her parents, her aunts and uncles, her strange cousin and his children. He had done what the others did, as far as he could figure out; he had dressed as the others did, ate as they ate, swam when they swam, slept when they slept. He had even, after a hissed reproach or two, kept his distance. It wasn't right "for that sort of thing," she told him, and he pretended to understand what she was talking about.

He had laughed at their jokes, when he understood them.

He had pitched in with the chores, joined in the games, and refrained from winning too many of them. He had caught a fish. He had participated in the discussions about the horrible traffic coming up.

And yet they insisted on serving him breakfast in bed.

After the first one, he tried to decline the second, saying he wanted to get up and greet the day, see what the birds were up to, perhaps do a bit of chopping. But they insisted. He ate his breakfast. It was very good and it took him a while to get through it. By the time he was dressed and out of the house, the others were halfway through the chores, which seemed to consist of taking boards and moving them from one place to another.

When he appeared, they were on to the next stage, which consisted of taking a few steps back from a spot and looking at it in an appraising manner. The woman didn't glare at him. She smiled absently and treated him as if he were not there. This was only the third day of his stay and she seemed more interested in what her aunt had to say about the coming weather than in what he had to say about what he knew about different varieties of moss. And yet they were supposed to be getting married, although they had not decided exactly when. Deciding would be a mere formality, just like meeting the relatives, she had said.

"What if they don't like me?" he had said.

"How could they not like you?" she had asked, and the conversation ended there, with him not being able to think of anything. Somehow, now, everything had gone wrong.

He had praised the town when he arrived. He had praised the boat, praised the water, praised the cottage, praised the food, praised the trees, even praised a bat that flew by at dusk. He had gone for a swim and said the water was just right, even though it felt very cold. He had declined a third helping. He had offered to help with the dishes. He had been understanding about not trying anything funny, once she explained it to him.

"Maybe they don't like me," he said, on the fourth day.

"Don't be silly," she said, but then didn't add the part about how could anybody not like him.

"Maybe I should go back in a couple of days," he said, on the sixth day.

"Don't be silly," she said. "They adore you. Look how they always bring you breakfast in bed."

"I think I'll go back tomorrow," he said, on the eighth day.

"I wish you could stay," she said, "but I know you've got things to do."

✳   ✳   ✳

Why do people not fit in? Why does one lover spend a week at the other lover's cottage and become an ex-lover? Situations vary. Some relationships are more deeply rooted than others. Some relationships need electricity. Relatives can become troubling. Some relationships never survive outdoor plumbing. Those variations aside, reasons for the breakup of relationships at the cottage can be listed. Not all apply in all situations. For more convenient analysis, the reasons have been divided into two categories, male and female. Other categories would complicate matters unnecessarily.

Male
Looks "wrong" holding a crowbar.
Got into a canoe backwards the first time.
Apologizes too much.
Wears matching outfits.
Says "perhaps" when talking in the woods.
Spends too long discussing bridge hand instead of dealing the next one.
Talked about "leveraged buyout situation" over supper.
Brought recipe involving green noodles.
Talks about the lake where he spent summers as a child.
Brought two kinds of suntan lotion.

Became too excited about sunset.
Brought green noodles.
Insists on breakfast in bed.

Female
Wears baseball cap with name of Toronto restaurant on it.
Cheats at Monopoly.
Talks about the lake where she spent her summers as a child.
Tries too hard to make little kids like her.
Says "goddamn" too much.
Brought transistor radio and keeps trying to find the CBC on it.
Says pickerel fillets are "to die for."
Brought magazines.
Smokes little cigars.
Looks funny holding dishcloth.
Ran boat at slow speed into concealed rock nobody had warned her about. Said "sorry" many times and no damage done, but still . . .
Insists on breakfast in bed.

✻ ✻ ✻

One night, early in the second week, she was sitting on the veranda minding her own business, half watching the sunset and half trying to read a book by what was left of the light. She enjoyed the quiet, the first she'd had all day. People had been yelling at her to do things differently, first in the boat, then in the woods; the children had been nagging at her to play some stupid game she had invented and then forgotten about.

Then the crabby uncle – or at least the one she thought was the crabbiest – said: "If you'll get me a cup of coffee I'll save your seat." She sighed, got up, got the coffee, came back, and the seat was gone. The uncle laughed, and the cousin who was in the seat laughed too.

She found another seat and went back to the book. The nightly bridge game began and she was not invited to join it. When she decided to turn in, nobody did more than look up and mutter something. The next morning, at eight-thirty, one of the little kids hammered on her head with a pillow and one of the aunts told her that if she didn't get out of bed soon all the breakfast would be gone.

She dragged herself up, dressed, and got to the table in time to see most of the others there. They said it was about time she showed up. The man who had brought her there just smiled. She realized she was a good camper.

Part 6

The Outside World

Town

Still Not the City

In Town, there used to be old-timers who knew everything. Town might have been a tiny village or a large town or almost a city. Town might have been merely a marina with a store in it. Whatever it was, it was Town. As in: "If you're going to Town, will you mail these letters?" Or: "Can I go to Town, Mommy, and get an ice cream cone?"

You would get in the boat or the car or on your bike and go to town and you would undoubtedly run into an old-timer. Old-timers were always there, dispensing lore, product information, and practical advice. Many of the things that were done at the cottage were done because an old-timer recommended that they be done that way. Many a lotion, an ointment, a glue, a wax was purchased for the cottage because an old-timer said it was the thing to use.

If you needed to know whether minnows were working this year, whether to use spiral or galvanized nails, or what mosquito repellent was best, the old-timer knew. From his perch in the hardware store, or at the dock, or even the post office, the old-timer would answer the question and ask after your family, sometimes confusing your generation with the one before it, or the one after.

This was despite the fact that he only saw you for two, three weeks, or a month a time. You always came back and he was always there. One year he wasn't there, but his son or daughter was, and the post of old-timer passed on to the next generation and was maintained.

A lot has changed, some of it for the better. Where you used to have to search the lake for a doctor on holidays, now there is a clinic in Town. True, there may be bloodstains leading up the front walk, but inside all is calm and efficient, and the prevalent malady – usually swimmer's ear – is swiftly diagnosed and prescribed for, and swiftly healed.

Other improvements include summer refrigeration. Blocks of ice are no longer necessary; milk can be stored for longer periods, more than three quarts at a time. The all-important propane and kerosene are more accessible; no longer are they dealt from someone's back yard, ten miles inland. Treated wood has been invented, and the road to the lake has been upgraded.

But there are counterbalances to weigh. The upgraded road brings more people, passing through. Without knowing the old-timer, they take up his time. The old-timer loses track of who the regulars are.

Once, there were fewer regulars. They were rich and easily spotted. But now, the huge, beautiful wooden mansions towering over the lake have seen divorces and family disagreements. The old summer estates have been split up, rented out, sold. Those who come back to them every summer no longer look like mansion-dwellers. They look like anyone else. The old-timer has trouble picking them out.

There are other changes. Big business has been invented and small business in Town faces extinction. The dairy is gone; so is the bakery. A giant air-conditioned and odourless super-market has been invented. Portable music has been invented, as well as bigger boats. Bigger government has been invented, decreeing that those boats be equipped with horns. The boats use them. The lake is cluttered with rules and signs telling people what the rules are. There are rules that never existed in the old-timer's day, such as the one saying you have to carry a whistle in a canoe.

An arsenal of sprays has been invented, to keep various things under control. Summer smells like Raid. The old-timer will comment on this and other matters if you can find him. He is a little harder to spot these days. In the hardware store, a customer asks for advice on bug sprays. The man behind the counter offers only the information that can be found in advertising, or on the back of the can. There is no old-timer there who would know for sure. The customer, to be on the safe side, buys one of each brand. In the sporting goods store – the one that used to be called a tackle shop, but now sells mostly leisure outfits – a customer asks what the tourists are buying.

The old-timer, of course, knew not only what the tourists were using but what the guides were using; knew what the big muskie was caught on last week. He also knew where it was caught. It was said that he knew what the Indians knew, so the regulars knew what the Indians knew too.

The Indians and the old-timers used to sit on benches and exchange information in the grassy places near the lake. Now those places are paved over for parking lots and glassy offices where realtors and lawyers watch the value of the land go up and decide when to sell and when to buy more. People sit and talk in the shopping centres, but it is not the same, and old-timers are not at home there.

Town is still not exactly like the city. A woman can breast-feed a child while strolling down a supermarket aisle without causing a stir or violating seven separate bylaws. Cheques can still be cashed in Town, charge accounts reopened from summer to summer, and the library may still not fine for overdue books. In Town, there is a lingering element of mutual trust that the city may have lost. But the warning signs are out. One of them is that the cottagers are more self-reliant – or think they are. In an era of mass communication, they learn from books and consumer magazines and television, and think they don't need the old-timer any more. The locally made gunk that keeps the mosquitoes away has been tested and analyzed by a national publication and found to be more expensive, on a unit-cost basis, than a mass-produced product.

The sporting goods store, the one that used to be the tackle shop, will disappear next year. Sporting goods will be available in a small corner of the department store in the shopping centre. The post office, where they used to know everybody's name, now has ropes for people to stand behind while they wait in line, and children need a signed note to pick up their parents' mail. It is a busy place and there is no time to chat. One of the docks has been converted into a restaurant. The hardware store has become a Canadian Tire, and there is no old-timer in it.

The old-timer is becoming a thing of the past.

News

The Landscape Is Strong

Once there, Cottage Man's priorities change. The important things are:

The water: Is there enough of it? Is the pump working? Is it clean? Is the level up or down? Has the algae arrived yet? Is it too soupy to swim in?

The bugs: How bad are they this year? Are those biting flies about to go away, or are they just starting? What about spraying for the mosquitoes? Is that going to harm anything other than the mosquitoes?

The beasts: Are raccoons around? Has anybody seen bears? Are the muskrats eating the styrofoam? Can the dog learn to ignore the squirrels? Does anybody know what made those droppings on the path?

The weather: Will it ever warm up? Will it ever cool off? Has there ever been so much rain?

The trees: Are all the spruces going to die? What's happening to the birches? What are we going to do about that big dead pine? Will it fill the wood shelter if we cut it up?

The fish: Are they biting? If so, are they edible, or are they full of mercury?

For three weeks of his life, Cottage Man lives close to nature

–maybe not right there, exactly, but closer than he usually gets. Elements of his closeness to nature matter to him. They matter more than the stock market, more than memos, more than Parliament, more, even, than pennant races.

By city terms, Cottage Man is "away from it all." By his own terms, Cottage Man is not away from it; he is *at* it. City stuff takes on, in his mind, an irrelevance. He can't understand how he allowed his stomach to churn over trying to find a parking spot. He vows not to let it happen again and resolves to sort out his fall and winter priorities. Meanwhile, the pump is making a funny sound.

Cottage Man watches, from a world that seems real to him, the so-called Real World go by. Except for special occasions, he watches through newspapers, when someone remembers to pick one up. Television ceases to exist. A special occasion is man's first landing on the moon. He listens, on the radio at dusk, to one giant leap for mankind, then goes to fill the kerosene lamps. He remembers various summer Olympics only by what he read about them in the newspapers. He recalls that the water level was high the year of the Montreal Olympics. When the so-called Real World impinges on his consciousness, it must compete for his attention. Even the political junkie – the one who has been known to discuss redistribution in the canoe – has difficulty keeping his mind on politics at the cottage. Following an election during the summer is an exercise in divided attention. From the cottage constituency, here's how the election looks:

Day One: Saying election is main concern, prime minister calls election. In unprecedented sighting, two pelicans spotted off beach. Main concern: why are pelicans there?

Day Two: Golf course scorecard says ball stolen by fox can be replaced without penalty. Golfer figures that fox worth four or five strokes over a summer. Paper quotes Opposition leader: "We are going in as the underdog." Four eagles sighted over bay.

Day Three: Dollar drops. Leaning white pine near dock leaning more decidedly. Main concern: cut white pine down or pull it up?

Day Four: Sliced drive ricochets off another white pine onto fairway where not stolen by fox. Three party leaders win nominations.

Day Five: Prime minister says he would like to be judged on his own performance. Outhouse moved to new location, which mosquitoes find. Thunderstorm arrives. Main concern: tent doesn't leak.

Day Six: Paper says Canadian bald eagles being exported to U.S. New poll shows government lead down to 2.5 per cent. White pine falls into water, ending Day Three debate.

Day Seven: Opposition leader accuses PM of swiping Opposition environment policy. Saskatoon berries appear, but in small numbers.

Day Eight: Inflation rate dips. Fallen tree is attacked from rowboat by willing workers armed with axes and saws. One attacker inadvertently struck by oar. Opposition leader says inflation should have dipped more.

Day Nine: Rabbit spotted at outhouse. Wind and cloud drive sunbathers inside, where they are forced to read newspapers. Main concern: Expos win; Jays lose. In other news, parties agree to TV debates, which will be fun to read.

Day Ten: Spruce too wet, birch too green, and boardwood too hot for wood stove. Energy minister announces decision not to run. Respected columnist notes damaging statements made by Opposition leader and urges him not to make any more statements. Expos lose; Blue Jays win. Angler finds large pike on his line, hauls it in, kills it, brings it home, and fillets it; forgets about prime minister, Opposition leader, and respected columnist for rest of day.

Day Eleven: Opposition leader unveils agriculture policy. Big white pine lying dead in forest yields stove wood and much-needed chopping blocks. Local weekly runs picture of retiring energy minister on page one, but below the fold. Above fold are two large pictures of Knights of Columbus picnic.

Day Twelve: Someone forgets to pick up the newspapers. Choppers laud new chopping blocks.

Day Thirteen: Heckler, approaching prime minister, is steered away by bodyguards. Prime minister says people are reaching out to him. Baby bear spotted gambolling among cottages on mainland. Main concern: whereabouts of mother bear.

Day Fourteen: Visiting expert offers fishing advice: worms, not minnows, fished deep. Top officials in Prairie riding jump from Tories to Liberals, or Liberals to Tories. Something like that. Worm shortage is main concern.

Day Fifteen: Weekend guest has been listening to car radio and brings word on television coverage of declining dollar. Woman laundering a few clothes by hand drops soap off end of dock. Main concern: soap doesn't float.

Day Sixteen: Pelican flies over dock. Fishing boat runs out of gas. Disappointing discovery made that oarlocks in fishing boat are defective. Outside world awaits French-language debate by party leaders.

Day Seventeen: Kerosene lamps lit and boat covered, in anticipation of storm, as candidates, heard on radio, debate interest rates, high technology, and environment. All say they will be announcing specific programs some time. Non-exported bald eagle appears at midafternoon. American symbol sits atop highest tree and squeaks when attacked by seagulls.

Day Eighteen: Paper runs comments of experts who say prime minister misspoke in debate. Storm narrowly misses golf course.

Day Nineteen: Intriguing two-man fishing technique observed in remote part of lake. One swims on surface with snorkel and mask to locate fish. Other casts. Results inconclusive. Election debate analysis continues: prime minister lost but won by not losing by as much as it was predicted he might. Weather sunny and warm.

Day Twenty: Worm and sinker method fails but ancient canoe, newly mended, floats and hardly leaks. Mouse traps self in can of bacon fat and has to be destroyed. PM apologizes for misquoting Opposition leader. Opposition leader demands further apology.

Day Twenty-One: Wind reappears after three-day absence; welcomed by windsurfers. Promised meteorite shower escapes view. Poll says key to election is vote of "ordinary Canadians." Ordinary Canadians debate fate of mouse.

Day Twenty-Two: Another poll gives government large lead, but poll was two weeks ago. Expert statisticians quoted on significance of this. Wind disappears. So does sun. Plague of tiny toads threatens.

Day Twenty-Three: PM shuffles top campaign officials. People step carefully to avoid tiny toads. Main concern: first bat in two years flies into veranda.

Day Twenty-Four: Absence of newspapers condemned by political junkie. Political junkie scolded for failing to applaud maiden solo shopping mission of pre-teen children. Absence of newspapers more than compensated for by presence of four new flavours of Jell-O.

Day Twenty-Five: Bald eagle, the American symbol, absent, but two beavers appear. Canadian symbols dive quietly without slapping their tails upon noticing people nearby. Opposition leader promises something having to do with armed forces.

Day Twenty-Six: While politicians sleep, northern lights chase each other across the sky at 3 A.M., accompanied by a shooting star and the voices of several insomniac loons. Prime minister, upon awakening, announces youth training program.

Day Twenty-Seven: Mystery bird sighted. Bird book reveals it to be a cormorant (immature). Ontario premier enters election debate by announcing that his province will stand by its usual policy, whatever that is. Boaters, at 3 A.M., awaken cottagers by carrying on loud conversation. Main concern: which way is north?

Day Twenty-Eight: Television network poll, taken after leaders' debate, shows all parties gaining. Seems plausible enough. Another American symbol, giant cabin cruiser, anchors just off beach, after occupants ask permission. Town celebrates bicentennial; celebrations enlivened by one jet and two waterbombers.

Day Twenty-Nine: Cottage Man heads for civilization. Bear stands beside highway to airport and so-called Real World. In Real World, television network says three party leaders did not campaign today. Cottage Man tries to sleep, notes noise of traffic and absence of loons. Election has three weeks to go. Cottage Man begins to worry about it.

The Marina

No Place for a Boat

The marina began as a gas pump on the dock. Now it sells sailboats, CanLit, black noodles, tennis togs, and gelato. The lake didn't seem to change while the gas pump turned into a marina, but it probably did.

When the marina just sold gas, it was not called a marina. Nobody had ever heard of the word *marina*. If, sometime after the war, you drove your boat up to the gas pump on the dock and asked if this was the marina, the guy at the pump would have looked at you strangely and said: "Never heard of her."

There would then follow, as often followed in those days, a long discussion on words and names that sounded like *marina*. There was a lot more time, in those days, to discuss such matters at the gas pump on the dock because life was simpler, the pace was slower, there was quite a bit less gourmet cooking, and nobody was waiting impatiently back at the cottage for you to show up with the black noodles.

Asking for black noodles would have elicited a similar response. In those days, black noodles were thought of as just noodles that got dirty somehow, perhaps by falling into the grease in the boat repair shop that was behind the gas pump.

The gas pump and boat repair shop wasn't the only gas

pump and boat repair shop. The waterfront had several. This was when boats had smaller gas tanks and had to fill up more frequently. And it was before land-owners discovered that huge amounts of money could be made by buying up waterfront property and not doing anything with it. It is an axiom of vacation-land real estate that the value of land appreciates all the more the less is done with it. This is because it has terrific potential. As soon as something is done to it, such as making it into an antique shop, the terrific potential is gone. It becomes an antique shop, and therefore of less value than a vacant lot to someone who doesn't want to own an antique shop.

So now the waterfront in cottage towns is comprised equally of lawyers' offices, real estate offices, and vacant lots. Plus the marina.

The marina, if it is really nice and owned by a human being rather than a numbered corporation, may store your boat for you over the winter. This is something that the old gas pump and boat repair shop always did. And if your boat, next spring, looked like it had been badly treated, if it was scratched and the insides were littered with things that looked like black noodles, you could always take your business to another gas pump.

The gas pump and boat repair shop also pumped kerosene for you out of a pump at the back. It fixed your boat and provided a taxi boat to take you where you needed to go while your boat was being fixed, or if somebody really important was coming to visit you and would be wearing good clothes. It was axiomatic a few years back that no man wearing a tie or woman wearing a hat should be met in an outboard. It would have to be the taxi boat, which was covered and elegantly slow in the water.

Back from the pumps was the boat repair shop, a huge barn-like place with four slips. The slips were full of boats, and other boats hung from the ceiling. Swallows flew around inside. While your boat was being fixed, you could wander around and look at the other boats and listen to the swallows. You could examine the range of products available for sale. These consisted of:

Small green bottles of Coca-Cola, out of a machine.

Cans of 10W 30 motor oil.

Cans of 10W 40 motor oil.

Plus the world's smallest selection of fishing gear, consisting of three spinners, five leaders, two sinkers, and a reel of black fishing line.

The old guy who ran the place wasn't really an old guy at all. He was probably forty-five. But he looked old to you, because he was a grownup and covered with grease and you were a kid and covered with Coca-Cola. The old guy had kids too, who helped out, fetching wrenches and oily rags, and whom you envied.

It was when one of those kids grew up and became a partner in the business that the gas pump and boat repair shop started on the slippery slope down towards marina-hood. First, a part of the boat repair shop was done over into a little store, for the convenience, mostly, of fishermen. The supply of plugs and spinners was increased. Multicoloured fishing line was placed in stock. A live bait tank was purchased and filled with minnows and crayfish. Worms appeared, and the variety of soft drinks was increased, although there was no reason to suspect a link between the two.

Fishermen also needed coffee and tea, so coffee and tea were put on sale. The next step after that was milk, and before long families were stopping in to pick up the things they had forgotten to bring from the city.

None of this necessarily guaranteed that marina status was inevitable. It began to be so, however, when one of the new owners started hiring outside the family. Instead of installing his own kids at the pumps, he hired some of the local teen-age boys. As luck would have it, they were teen-age boys of the type found attractive by teen-age girls. The owner also hired teen-age girls, of a type found attractive by teen-age boys, to work the cash in the store. Soon, teen-agers were hanging around the gas pumps, loitering in the store, and playing with the live bait. The gas pump and boat repair shop had become an event.

Still, it wasn't making much money. Boats were getting bigger, so were their tanks, and fewer of them were stopping. The owners of the boats were carrying more and more supplies and the supplies were increasingly of a type – herbs and liqueurs, fashion magazines and No. 32 sunscreen – that had to be purchased in urban centres before the boat's voyage began. When boaters did stop, their requests were odd: a zucchini, a spare set of backgammon dice, some stained glass. As for milk, bread, and sinkers, people were getting those at the Loblaws that had opened up where one of the old gas pumps and boat repair shops used to be.

The gas pump and boat repair shop, which had now become the gas pump and convenience store, had a choice now: to become the marina or go out of business. When it became the marina, it forgot how to repair boats, but boat owners were hitching the boats onto trailers and towing them somewhere up on the highway to be fixed anyway. The marina owners learned to stock paperbacks, cookbooks, city magazines, spices, cat food, and video movies, VHS and Beta – all the new staples of cottage life.

So there it is – the marina. The gas pump is still there and so are the teens who hang around it. Certain of the more popular movies will be gone unless you rent them by Thursday noon. Olive oil is on special. Any of those sailboats over there is for rent. And if you are thinking of buying one, you can visit the showroom out back, where they used to pump the kerosene.

The Yacht Club

A Good Time But Not Grand

As far as anyone can remember, there has never been a yacht near the place. Yet it's called the yacht club. Even when it is not named the yacht club, officially, even when it's called the Muddy Lake Recreational and Cultural Association (MLRCA), they still call it the yacht club.

One day, as you picture it, a big boat stopped at the site of what is now the yacht club and rich people got out, the men in white flannels, carrying one of those large straw baskets –

No, wait a minute. The rich men in the white flannels weren't carrying the large straw baskets. They had servants, who got out of the big boat, then helped them out so they wouldn't get their white flannels dirty, then carried the large straw baskets so they could have their picnic right there.

That would be a good explanation for it, why it came to be known as the yacht club. That boat with the guys in the white flannels, plus the women with the long dresses and bonnets, the servants and the ukuleles – that was a big boat, and maybe it was a yacht.

When the club was established, back when rich people on the lake were really rich and you could tell, the club had lots of big boats tied up to it. And maybe the rich people – the swells, they were called – liked the idea of having something called the yacht club.

So it stays that way now, even though there are no yachts, just a fairly large cabin cruiser that one of the members bought sort of by mistake. It was a mistake because he didn't know about boats and thought he should buy the biggest and most expensive one in the showroom, although, as it turned out, he would never go more than half a mile in it, and the bunks in the cabins were used only every once in a while as an enticement to the children to take afternoon naps, and then only when the boat was safely tied to the dock. The boat is so nice and so expensive that the owner is afraid to take it the half mile to the marina. So he bought an old aluminum putt-putt, as he calls it, and keeps the big one for trips to the yacht club, where the children admire it and the grownups resent it.

That boat comes to the yacht club, plus some speedboats and some fairly large sailboats. But you wouldn't call any of them yachts.

A few years ago, the members of the yacht club decided that it was silly to call their yacht club a yacht club when it didn't have any yachts. It became the Muddy Lake Recreational Association (MLRA). The present name, the Muddy Lake Rec-reational and Cultural Association, came the summer after the book club was formed and met frequently at the yacht club (for it was still called the yacht club). There were book club members on the executive and they said there was more to a yacht club than merely recreation. There was culture, too. Since there were plans to augment the cultural aspect of the yacht club with lessons in French and yoga, there was little objection to the proposed name change, although some of the sailors grumbled a bit.

Compared to the days when it was really a yacht club, the MLRCA has fallen on hard times. Not that it is decrepit or cash poor. The place keeps itself afloat on T-shirt sales alone. Mem-bership dues help, and the bake sales bring in a fair amount of money, enough to pay the swimming instructors, the sailing coach, the tennis pro, and the disk jockey. Still . . .

The dances are not what they were when the men wore white flannels. They say that there was always a band, a big one, with trumpets and trombones and saxophones. They say that Duke Ellington, or Cab Calloway, or somebody very much like that, once played at the yacht club. People danced around and sipped champagne, and their servants came and took them home, but well after midnight.

Now Saturday nights at the Muddy Lake Recreational and Cultural Association are taken up with the showing of two-year-old movies, and somebody has to look at them carefully to make sure there isn't too much sex in them for the children. The dances are held only twice a summer, and without a band. They feature – if that is the word – a nineteen-year-old disk jockey who gets $25 a night and thinks he deserves more. He sulks while he plays tapes of the *Big Chill* sound track and the kids watch their parents do the twist or the hully-gully or one of those old dances, whatever they were called. There is no liquor, except out in the bushes, because the executive is safety-conscious and doesn't want harm to befall anyone on the lake after dark. There is coffee and lemonade and various baked goods that the members bring.

Everyone has a good time. It just is not that grand any more. Everybody belongs to the yacht club now, except for the people who refuse to join anything, so there is no exclusivity to it, and it is a sure thing that the people who really have yachts, if there really are such people, go somewhere else.

Mind you, the people around the MLRCA have better things to do than spend their time pining away for lost yachts. They are busy with a wide variety of classes and lessons. A person can spend a lot of useful time during the summer at the yacht club, learning how to do this and that. And it is a good place to dump, or send, the children, so that they do not waste their summers just having fun. They can learn to sail or play tennis or tie knots. There may be yoga lessons for children soon.

One year there were accordion lessons, which were educational, although there was only one accordion and it had to be passed around. The next year, just when everybody was looking forward to advanced, or at least intermediate, accordion lessons, the accordion teacher failed to appear. And since it was his accordion, that was that.

Aerobics have become a popular activity, and the club is thinking of purchasing a set of weights for people to wear around their ankles while working out. There is a degree of controversy about this, centring mainly on what is seen as a choice between the ankle weights or some archery equipment. Those in favour of the archery equipment say that their sport is healthy and takes place in the out-of-doors. The ankle weight supporters say that archery lacks benefit to the heart and lungs, and anyway an arrow might get away and put someone's eye out.

The dispute will probably be settled without lasting damage to the yacht club Spirit. A more divisive issue is the one that arises each year in preparation for the regatta. It concerns the awarding of trophies. The dispute is between those who want to encourage a high level of participation and those who want to encourage a high level of competition. The latter group, which numbers among its members the best sailors, rowers, swimmers, canoeists, and tennis players – for all are included in the regatta, along with checkers, chess, and, for the first time this year, aerobics – thinks trophies should only be awarded to those who finish first, second, and third in various competitions.

Each year, the statement of their position is met with groans and mutters of outrage from those who do not canoe, swim, sail, row, or play checkers all that well, and whose children do not either.

"It's all right for *you* to favour a high level of competition," someone is bound to say. "You already *have* lots of trophies."

That person will go on to say, as he does every summer, that excessive competitiveness can be psychologically damaging, and that every child, notwithstanding his station in life and athletic abilities, has a right to a trophy or two each summer.

This view has tended to prevail, helped along by the discovery of a cheap trophy supplier.

After the regatta is over and hundreds of trophies have been duly awarded, the yacht club slows its activities to a crawl, and only a few of its members actively nurture the hope that the yacht club, some day, may again be a place where yachts might go.

The Association

A Question Deferred Until Next Summer

The cottagers association meets at the yacht club, except once in a while when one of the members of the executive has just finished renovations to his cottage and wants everyone to see it. When the executive of the cottagers association meets at the yacht club, it is difficult to tell it from the executive of the Muddy Lake Recreational and Cultural Association. They are pretty well the same people, and when they meet in the same place people have to be on their toes to remember which meeting they are having.

Someone is always wanting to discuss the next dance or the purchase of some recreational or cultural equipment, and being declared out of order for discussing it, if the chairperson is alert enough to spot the discrepancy.

Most of the time, the topics of discussion are quite serious, because they don't meet very often and so a lot of serious things have happened between times, which are saved up for the meetings. The only non-serious issue members can remember – and it seemed pretty serious at the time – was the business of where the apostrophe in "cottagers association" should go, the question turning on the differing definitions, among members of the executive, of what constituted a singular and what a plural.

When the matter was put to the executive, it split between the doctrinaire grammarian faction and the abstractionist group. The former said that many cottagers were involved in the association and the association was for all of them, so it should be called a cottagers', plural, association. The abstractionist group – defined by their enemies as people who not only can't start their boat but often can't find it – thought the association was representative of a symbolic cottager who stood for them all, and therefore should be a cottager's, singular, association.

This took up much of one afternoon, which, fortunately, was rainy anyway. When discussion had just about run out and it looked like it was time to put the question, someone else, a man who had fled Montreal in the late seventies, remembered that there the apostrophes had been taken off everything in a move that had something to do with French. The Eaton's store had become the Eaton store and so on. Not that he was condoning separatism or anything, the man from Montreal said, but wouldn't that simplify matters to name the cottager's or cottagers' association in like fashion?

There was a moment of confusion, followed by an argument about whether or not it would sound silly to call it the cottager association. Finally, the treasurer spoke up, a woman everybody respected because she balanced the books well, had an old 10-horsepower Evinrude and could fix it herself.

"No matter where we put the apostrophe," she said, "people are going to get it wrong. Let's not have any. Just call it the cottagers, no apostrophe, association."

This led to considerably more debate, but, in the end, the treasurer's view prevailed. It was now the cottagers, no apostrophe, association, and for a while people called it that, shortened eventually to the CNAA.

Most of the time, as the following minutes show, discussion was on more serious topics:

Minutes of the CNAA

August 4

C. Maxwell (Chairperson), R. Parrish (Sec-Treas), H. Luisetti (Deputy Chairperson), L. Bucyk (Sergeant-at-Arms). 36 Others.

The meeting began at 3:12 P.M. The Chairperson welcomed the members, particularly on such a sunny day. The minutes of the last meeting were deferred and would be approved when they are presented at the next meeting. The Secretary said she was sure she would be able to locate them.

The Treasurer's report, which said the association was in a surplus position, was warmly applauded. Ms Parrish, in her capacity as Chairperson of the Sub-Committee on Archival Matters, said the extra money could be put to good use for electric typewriter ribbons and good quality paper for the history of the Association, upon which she was embarked. Some discussion followed on this, with a man at the back of the room saying it was his understanding that the Association was only seven years old and maybe it might be a good idea to wait a longer period of time before writing a history of it. Ms Parrish replied that the history of the Association was approved at the last meeting, as the minutes would show when they are available. Mr. McHale said the use of the surplus should be put to a referendum of the membership. Mr. Jones asked how much the surplus was, exactly, and the Treasurer promised to get back to him on that.

Under Old Business, the question of the houseboats was reviewed. The Houseboat Watchdog Committee, under Ms Parrish, reported that, in the month of July, 89 houseboats were counted, although some of them might have been the same one going out and then coming back, and there were times when she was busy and could only keep one eye out for them. The Chairperson asked if this was an increase or a decline over the last month and the Secretary promised to get back to him on that when last month's minutes were located.

With regard to houseboats, Mrs. Roberts, a new member, said that she had once toured the lake in one several years ago before buying her cottage. The Chairperson of the Houseboat Watchdog Committee asked Mrs. Roberts if she was aware of the terrible noise and clatter that were made and the disgraceful substances that were flushed into or dumped onto the water by houseboats. Mrs. Roberts said that she couldn't vouch for the other houseboaters but that she and her husband would never do anything like that themselves. The Chairperson informed Mrs. Roberts of an incident in which he personally had witnessed houseboaters shouting and voiding late at night.

The Social Committee, under Mr. Bucyk, reported that another Square Dance would be held before Labour Day. There was some discussion as to why there could not be some other form of music at these dances. Mr. Bucyk said that it had always been a tradition at the yacht club to hold Square Dances, but he realized that this was a Cottagers Association meeting, not a Yacht Club meeting, and perhaps it was not the right time to discuss this.

Mrs. Roberts spoke again and mentioned that she had heard about a developer who might be interested in the old McAuley property up the lake and was going to put a 15-storey high-rise hotel on it with a five-storey parking garage. The Chairperson said that should come under New Business. The Treasurer asked Mrs. Roberts where she would get a ridiculous story like that from and Mrs. Roberts said she couldn't help it, that was what she had heard. The Chairperson appointed Mrs. Roberts a Sub-Committee to investigate and report back to the CNAA at the next meeting.

The Water Testing Committee (Ms Parrish) reported that the levels were the same as last time, which was not good news, but could be worse. Mrs. Roberts spoke from the floor, asking if anything could be done about these water levels, which were lower than when she bought her cottage and made it difficult for her parents to get out of the boat. The Chairperson of the Water Testing Committee said that this was not the job of the Water Testing Committee, which was to test the water for levels of bacteria and coliform count and not to measure how high it

was. She suggested that perhaps Mrs. Roberts might like to
volunteer to head up a Water Levels Committee, but Mrs.
Roberts declined, saying that she would have enough to do
being the Sub-Committee to investigate the new development
on the McAuley property.

The Speedboat Committee (Ms Parrish) reported that there
seemed to be one more on the lake than at this time last year,
but it may have been that one of the previous ones had been
painted. Mrs. Roberts asked why nothing could be done about
these speedboats. The Speedboat Committee Chairperson
replied that it was the policy of her Committee to phone the
Provincial Police at every opportunity, but the Police had informed her that no charges could be laid unless specific infrac-
tions could be detected.

Under New Business, the Chairperson said there had been
a suggestion that the Association have a Flag and a new logo to
better represent the Association's purposes and tradition. The
Chairperson said he knew a man in the city who made his living
at this kind of thing and might be able to give the Association
a reduced rate. This led to a discussion of the Association's
purposes, during which it was decided to adjourn and discuss
the topic at the next meeting.

Members were invited to participate in the First Annual
Cottage Tour the next Saturday, which it was hoped would
become an annual event. Following adjournment, light refresh-
ments were served.

All of which is respectfully submitted.

R. Parrish (Ms), Secretary

✳   ✳   ✳

All across the country, executive members of cottage owners
associations share a common bond—their determination to fight
the narrow-mindedness of the local authorities, who persist in
failing to recognize the legitimate rights and interests of the
summer community, particularly with regard to garbage pickup
and repairing the ruts in the dirt roads, despite the fact that the

members of the summer community have been law-abiding residents for years and regularly pay their taxes too.

All across the country, they count houseboats, hold meetings, raise funds by selling home-made quilts and cookies, and debate the design of the new logo. If that is supposed to be a loon in the upper left-hand corner, shouldn't it at least *look* like a loon? The question, like far too many questions, will have to be deferred until next summer.

The Cottage Tour

Coveting Thy Neighbour's Axe

Every year the association tries to take KenHel off the cottage tour, and every year Helen pleads until the association relents and puts it back on. Then every year Helen does something to ruin it again.

Helen and her husband Ken have put a lot into KenHel, their tiny island. They have restored the boathouse to its original condition. The main cottage looks, from the outside, just as it must have at the turn of the century when it was constructed. The Union Jack still waves from the flagpole, the way it did. Except for the name – it used to be called Round Island, and still is on the map as such – nothing is different on the outside. And the fact that Helen and Ken have changed the name of the island doesn't mean they don't appreciate the island's history. They just wanted to make it more, somehow, personal.

Because of its tradition, every year KenHel is put on the cottage tour, along with Whistling Poplars, Bide-A-Wee, Rocky Point, Notre Tresoir, The Ferns, and Ka-Ba-Ki, the McIntosh place. The people who have bought their $10 tickets from the association are allowed to walk through it, look around a bit, scan the little pamphlet Ken and Helen have had printed up, and have a cup of tea. Some of the men look, as they do at all

the cottages, under the dock to see how it is supported. Then
it is off to the next island and the one after, plus a couple of the
nicer homes on the mainland, to gaze at everything from the
newest satellite dish to collections of early axes and hammers.

In the five years since the tour has been going on, the maps
have been improved, so much so that no boat has run up on
the rock in front of KenHel for quite a while. The worst thing
that has happened lately is that one boat ran up on Ken, who
was coming around the corner too fast in the opposite direction, after lunch at the yacht club. There is still the problem, at
KenHel, as elsewhere, of the missing spoons. Ken and Helen
have little tea spoons commemorating every royal visit since
1918, plus some from Expo '67 and one from the World's Fair
in Seattle. She brings them out with the tea every year, and
every year there are fewer left. There are still hundreds, though.
When Helen and the others on the cottage tour compare notes,
which they do very gingerly, not wanting to give away any
secrets, spoons are often mentioned.

Each cottage has its own character. Whistling Poplars has
the turn-of-the-century gazebo, sitting beneath where the
poplars used to be before they were cut down by beavers. Bide-
A-Wee has the marlin or swordfish or whatever it is hanging
over the mantelpiece. Every year someone asks about the marlin, trying delicately to avoid saying, out and out, that a stuffed
swordfish is out of place at a cottage on a freshwater lake. If
Mr. Bide-A-Wee is around when the question is asked – meaning
that he could not get a tee-off time – he will regale the group
with the complete story of his two-hour struggle, man against
fish, rod bent double, off Key West. If Mr. Bide-A-Wee is off
at the golf course, Mrs. Bide-A-Wee will tell the story of how
she bought the stuffed marlin at a garage sale.

Rocky Point has the wood stove, the ancient cooking uten-
sils, hammers, and axes, and the small museum depicting the
cottage's entire history, from the first owner to the present ones,
since it was first constructed, in 1956.

Notre Tresoir, which means something in French, according

to its owners, and they would never change it, has the huge fireplace and brightly polished set of brass fireplace implements. The owners are rightly proud of the fireplace and always have a fire burning brightly in it, even though some find this custom a bit warm for mid-July, when the cottage tour is often held.

The Ferns has just been taken over by some nice people from the city who have decorated it entirely in pastels. This year they served an unusual punch and had, someone noticed, risqué line drawings in the bathroom and, someone else noticed, perhaps the widest assortment of pills on the lake. There have been some questions as to why this cottage has been included on the tour, since it is neither very new nor very old, does not have famous owners, and lacks any history to speak of. The entry for The Ferns in the Annual Cottage Tour brochure only hints at this problem:

"Settled in 1949, The Ferns draws its evocative name from what is believed to be a beautiful bed of ferns sitting at approximately the spot where the tool shed is now.

"The cottage, located at the northwest corner of the island, is not the original cottage. The tool shed is, however, the original tool shed.

"The kitchen, partly remodelled in 1975, has many labour-saving devices and a nice view out the window.

"Future expansion of the tool shed is planned for next year."

The association treasurer says he helped write the brochure entry for The Ferns and will only smile when asked why it is on the tour this year.

KenHel has none of the pedigree problems of The Ferns. Its problem, if you want to call it a problem, is one of identity. Helen keeps buying new things for it, and wants to show them off. So once inside the beautifully preserved turn-of-the-century cottage, visitors must tour the kitchen, admiring the microwave oven and the stove with the indoor barbecue. They must see the complete set of herbs and spices, the salad dressings aligned in alphabetical order. Moving to the living room, they must see the new VCR, the home computer ("first on the lake with a hard disk," Ken will say, if he is home), and the state-of-the-art fire extinguisher.

This year's highlight is the fully automated multimedia tape and slide program that Helen has set up, with Ken's technical help. At the flip of a switch, the lights darken and the drapes close, a screen is lowered from the ceiling, and slides of summers past and present are projected upon it, with Ken and Helen pointing to various features, horsing around and holding up trophies, while the taped voices of Helen and Ken talk about their glorious association with the lake.

The slide show represents the first time that many of those present have seen Helen in a bikini, and the sight makes them anxious to feel their way out of the room, down the path and to the boat, ready – eager, even – to risk the rocks on the way out. As they depart, Ken's taped words ring in their ears:

"Those trophies are really something to behold, aren't they? And you know what I mean! Just kidding!"

Once past the rocks and out of the harbour, the relieved members of the association who still want to get their $10 worth motor over to Ka-Ba-Ki, apparently a Cree word meaning "random syllables."

Closing

*Good Riddance,
And When Can We Go Back?*

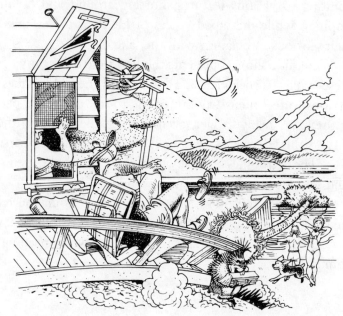

Closing

Good Riddance,
And When Can We Go Back?

Every single bit of food, every cookie, every sliver of cheese, every half-empty jar of somebody's home-made jam – all of it has to go. It has to be dumped into the garbage. Or it has to be carried to the boat or the car. The people doing the carrying are going to complain. This Labour Day, no labour feels less fruitful, while at the same time more hurtful to the back, than carrying boxes full of half-empty jars. But it all has to go. Leaving it around is an invitation to every beast of the forest to spend the winter in your cottage.

Sure, there is always the chance of coming back at Thanksgiving. But for the moment everyone remembers last Thanksgiving at the cottage – how the children complained about the cold, how the men spent all Saturday looking for a warm place to watch the baseball playoffs, how the women vowed never to listen to the complaining again. Better not to count on cleaning up the rest of it at Thanksgiving.

It is not easy work disposing of all that food. Nor is it appetizing. There are things at the back of the fridge that cannot be identified. They have lost their shape, their colour. They are covered with a coating of mould. Although there is a distinctive smell, it does not remind anybody of anything they ever wanted to eat.

The shutters have to come out from under the house. Under the house is full of spiderwebs, miscellaneous animal droppings, and beams that hit people on the head because they are lower than they used to be or the people bend over less well. Whoever stowed the shutters under the house in the spring did it all wrong, so that they are harder to get out this year than they ever were.

And that's not the half of it with the shutters. Once they are dragged out from under the house, they won't fit the windows and doors they are supposed to fit. ·

And although every year someone vows, when shutters are being taken off, to mark them with signs indicating the windows and doors from which they have come, no one got around to it this year. Everyone was in such a hurry to get warm, back in May, such a hurry to get inside near the fire.

Now the shutters have to go on. Some of them carry markings of a sort, a sign that previous generations were like-minded about shutter identification. But the markings don't mean anything. Or at least they don't mean what they once did. W6, one of them says, in what appears to be nail polish. That could be the sixth window on the west side. But the west side doesn't have any windows. And no side has six windows. Maybe a previous generation had a different idea of which direction is west. There were some weird things about some of those previous generations.

It is possible that the nail polish really says 9M. But that wouldn't mean much either. If one of the window frames had 9M marked on it, or even W6, that would help. But the markings on the window frames are in Roman numerals, undoubtedly the work of a great-great-uncle who was a Classics professor. The shutters go back that far, and every year the shutters have warped and bent a bit more. At this stage, even if people knew where the shutters were supposed to go, that would be no guarantee that they would actually go there.

Banging, hammering, and cursing accompany the installation of the shutters. There is a break for lunch, which consists of almost fresh bread, slivers of cheese, some red Kool-Aid, and some milk that might have stayed around a day too long. For dessert there are bruised apples and some vanilla ice cream that has crystallized in places. There wasn't much point, it is explained, in bringing up anything new from the city, since it would all have to be taken back anyway.

After lunch are packing and final chores. The women are grumpy because they are washing the floor. They don't understand why it is that they always get stuck washing the floor. The men are grumpy because they want to get on the road and beat the traffic. They can't understand why washing the floor is so important. They are especially grumpy because they know they won't beat the traffic. They would have had to have left three weeks ago at about 2 A.M. to beat the traffic.

It seems like only yesterday they were beating the traffic the other way, on the way up here, and it *was* only yesterday, or maybe the day before that. For that, and for the prospect of doing the drive again in an hour or so, they got two rainy days and a bit of one that was only cloudy. The water was too cold for anyone but children to swim in. The last good meal was the Burger King on the way up because all the food left in the fridge had to be finished off.

The children are grumpy because they have been told that if they can't find the new *Archie* comics they just bought, they will have to leave without them because no one is going to hold up the whole trip back to the city just for a comic book.

Everybody is grumpy. The clean-up takes too long. Taking the pump apart is impossible. Moving all the outdoor furniture inside is a pain in the neck. The water is too cold for a last swim. The comic books are never found. The dog decides to go for a swim and a roll around in the dirt just before getting into the car. It has been a terrible day so far. The car doors close, the car starts and begins to move towards the city. The worst is behind them. All the people in the car are in tears. They want to go back.

✳   ✳   ✳

Every person has a reason to hate the cottage. And every person has a reason to hate leaving it. There is regret at the fun being over. And there is regret at the fun never having started, at least not in the way you thought it would.

Every year, when thoughts turn to summer, thoughts turn to non-stop fun. It puts a lot of pressure on summer, having to live up to that. There is a summer of the mind that is part childhood memory, part beer commercial. The long drive home on Labour Day is the sadder for having to mull over, during the usual traffic delays, the knowledge that the summer of the mind, the summer of non-stop fun, will have to wait until next year.

A great one it will be, though. Every television commercial glimpsed, as the weather warms up in spring, shouts "fun!" Every memory of summer childhood is sweet. The people in the television commercials can't stop having fun even long enough to sleep. And as for sleeping, well, nudge-nudge. The grownups in memories of childhood never have allergies, insomnia, and outbursts of temper over mysterious dents on boats and the sudden disappearance of key ropes. The people in television commercials never have to blow their noses.

In the summer of the mind, as in the beer commercials, the waters are always calm. The fast boats and other gas-powered gadgets that speed by on the lake never make noise. The beer in television commercials never makes anybody sick. The neighbours in television commercials never complain. This year, it wasn't like that at all, but maybe next year it will be.

In the summer of the mind, the loons call, the fish bite. Even though the waters are calm, the sailboats and windsurfers always skim nicely across the calm waters and look pretty against the setting sun. It is difficult for a real live summer to live up to such expectations, and it rarely does, which is one reason why it is seen off with such regret. One more week, maybe only a couple of days more, and the summer might have fulfilled its promise.

But now there's no chance of that. Now there are only the usual memories of the usual kind of summer. The state-of-the-art septic system didn't work all that well, except for the light that went on to indicate something being wrong with it. There was the usual number of unwanted beasts, undeterred by dogs, mothballs, new screens, plastic bags, and a redoubled effort to put the lids on tight and keep everything in the refrigerator. The dock didn't float away this summer, but the boat should have, for all the use it was to anybody. A brand new deck of cards was lost for weeks, until someone found it in the refrigerator.

Something smelly got stuck in the chimney. Nobody wanted to find out whether it was a bird or not.

There was hardly any sign of fish. Maybe they were not healthy. The weeds were healthy. The only trees that seemed really healthy were the poplars, and the beavers were cutting them all down. The beavers were making the trees fall the wrong way, leading to concern over the health, mental and physical, of the beavers. And it raised the question of whether the responsibility of it was getting to them, being national symbols and all.

The new neighbours had a state-of-the-art sound system that never failed. They also had a complete collection of *Big Chill* records and some astonishingly clear recordings of wolf calls. Either that or there were wolves, which was just one more thing to worry about, especially with having to go outside because of the failure of the state-of-the-art septic system.

The people who stayed in the city, who lived all summer in the heat and the smog, who finally decided, after all these years, to break down and buy air-conditioning, and then found out there wasn't an air-conditioning unit for sale – wasn't even a *fan* for sale in the entire city – the city people might have been glad to see the end of summer, but the cottage people weren't, despite everything, despite the state-of-the-art septic system.

Despite everything, somehow they regretted leaving it,

regretted it being over. New speedboat records were being set right in front of the dock, a new and powerful breed of biting fly had chosen the area immediately around the dock for its proving grounds and seemed to have a particular affinity for suntan lotion. Someone, close by, was just learning to play the cello. Despite that, and despite the fact that the cottage had almost the identical telephone number to that of the only pediatrician on the lake, it was hard to leave it.

Not only that, but it was hard to get away from it. The traffic wasn't going anywhere. Somebody about seven cars ahead had decided to obey the speed limit. The result was chaos. People were having a hard time getting back to the city, and they didn't want to get back to what they were getting back to. Work. A federal election. Newspapers. Trying to find a parking space. For each person in the car there was a particular dread. School. The grownups remembered it: that uneasy feeling in the pit of the young stomach that began about the middle of August. Many adults still experienced the sensation – sympathetic Labour Day pains.

The children sat and watched the traffic not moving and knew the fear that all their friends, over the summer, would somehow, unbeknownst to them, have moved on to something new. Some new fad, some new way of behaving that would leave them behind. They would show up on the first day and be the *only person in the entire school* wearing that kind of shoes; they would be the only person in the entire school who didn't now hate the group the whole school loved in June.

The horror. The children couldn't even be distracted from the coming horror by an *Archie* comic, since the new one was somewhere back at the cottage. Suddenly, when the kids arrived at school and began telling about the things they enjoyed during their holidays, the absurdity, the absolute futility of their past two months would become clear to them. They would remember the things they enjoyed, the things they learned, but how could they explain it to their friends–that they saw a *woodpecker*, that they learned to recognize different kinds of *trees*? Probably their friends were learning about sophisticated things like cigarettes and new parts of the body.

It would be no consolation to have adults explain the situation. Adults would know that every child who went away saw a woodpecker. Every child who went away learned how to recognize trees. It was just that none of them would admit it. Years later, after escaping the tyranny of childhood, they would be strolling through the forest one day and discover that they could recognize trees. They would be able to point out woodpeckers to their own children.

But for the time being, around Labour Day, some of them would envy their city-bound friends, the friends who never got away, who saw all the new movies, heard all the new songs, learned all the new words. They weren't stuck at some cottage with their relatives and no television set.

Only later, years later, would that sense of grievance give way. It would happen about the time the children were no longer children, about the time they found themselves thankful there was nothing to do. One day they would find themselves totally bored and totally at peace in a cottage somewhere, and realize how lucky they were, and how lucky they had always been.

OTHER TITLES FROM
DOUGLAS GIBSON BOOKS

PUBLISHED BY McCLELLAND & STEWART LTD.

THE CANADA TRIP *by* Charles Gordon
Charles Gordon and his wife drove from Ottawa to St. John's to Victoria and back. The result is "a very human, warm, funny book" (*Victoria Times Colonist*) that will set you planning your own trip.
Travel/Humour, 6 × 9, 364 pages, 22 maps, trade paperback

THE GRIM PIG *by* Charles Gordon
The world of news is laid bare in this "very wicked, subversive book . . . it reveals more than most readers should know about how newspapers – or at least some newspapers – are still created. This is exceedingly clever satire, with a real bite." *Ottawa Citizen*
Fiction, 6 × 9, 256 pages, trade paperback

HOW I SPENT MY SUMMER HOLIDAYS *by* W.O.Mitchell
A novel that rivals *Who has seen the Wind*. "Astonishing . . . Mitchell turns the pastoral myth of prairie boyhood inside out." *Toronto Star*
Fiction, 5½ × 8½, 276 pages, trade paperback

PADDLE TO THE AMAZON: The Ultimate 12,000-Mile Canoe Adventure *by* Don Starkell *edited by* Charles Wilkins
From Winnipeg to the mouth of the Amazon by canoe! "This real-life adventure book . . . must be ranked among the classics of the literature of survival." *Montreal Gazette* "Fantastic." Bill Mason
Adventure, 6 × 9, 320 pages, maps, photos, trade paperback

PADDLE TO THE ARCTIC *by* Don Starkell
The author of *Paddle to the Amazon* "has produced another remarkable book" *Quill & Quire*. His 5,000-kilometre trek across the Arctic by kayak or dragging a sled is a "fabulous adventure story." *Halifax Daily News*
Adventure, 6 × 9, 320 pages, maps, photos, trade paperback

CRAZY ABOUT LILI: A Novel *by* William Weintraub
The author of *City Unique* takes us back to wicked old Montreal in 1948 in this fine, funny novel, where an innocent young McGill student falls for a stripper.
Fiction, 5½ × 8½, 272 pages, hardcover

THE QUOTABLE ROBERTSON DAVIES: The Wit and Wisdom of the Master *selected by* James Channing Shaw
More than eight hundred quotable aphorisms, opinions, and general advice for living selected from all of Davies' works. A hypnotic little book.
Non-fiction, 5¼ × 7, 176 pages, hardcover